WHEN POETRY WAS THE WORLD

M. G. Stephens

Spuyten Duyvil
New York City

For Richard Gray, FBA

Long ago was the then beginning to seem like now
As now is but the setting out on a new but still
Undefined way. That now, the one once
Seen from far away, is our destiny
No matter what else may happen to us...
    —John Ashbery

But more than that—since 'place' is not now more than activity—there is the questions of *all* terms of relationship, and of the possible continuities of that relationship in a *time* which is continuous and at all moments 'present'— else it never was.
    —Robert Creeley

I.

ANGELS ON SECOND AVENUE

The snow had buried Stuyvesant.
The subways drummed the vaults.
—Robert Lowell

ANGELS ON SECOND AVENUE

In June 1966 I found my first New York apartment. The flat was a half block away from St. Mark's Church in-the-Bowery, a place I would get to know a lot about shortly. It was a cold water flat, meaning that if I wanted a bath, I had to boil water on the stove in the various dime-store pots and pans I owned. The apartment consisted of three small rooms, with a bathtub in the kitchen, which was also the middle room and the one into which I entered after opening the front door when I returned from work at the end of the day. I had a grungy toilet in a corner of the backroom. Very quickly I acquired a mattress, some blankets and a pillow, a small record player for a stack of jazz records (mostly Thelonious Monk, my idol), a typewriter, a small table, and two chairs.

I had a bookcase made of boards and cinder blocks that I found on one of the Lower East Side streets at night, and these shelves were filled mostly with poetry books, Ashbery to Zukofsky. One book was a thoroughly foxed paperback of Donald Allen's *New American Poetry*. There were no more than a hundred books, maybe only fifty. (I never counted them.) The bookcase took up a corner space in the living room, which I jokingly called the parlor, channeling my Irish grandmother in Brooklyn.

I was twenty years old and I worked in the music library at the newly opened Lincoln Center. I was taking home, after taxes, around a hundred dollars a week, paid out to me at the end of the month. Beer cost about ninety-nine cents for a low-end economy six-pack, such as Ringnes or Old Milwaukee. I bought bulgur wheat and brown rice and lentils at a pulse shop on First Avenue, a small brown bag of such things costing only pennies. I regularly bought marble-faced inexpensive lined notebooks and ballpoint pens at local stationers or got them uptown on the West Side or went to a little shop along West 4th in the Village, where I also sometimes sold the man books when I had exceeded my measly budget and needed cash to get to work, to eat, and to buy beer and wine.

I also indulged in that writer's extravagance, a black spring binder, which every would-be poet seemed to possess, no matter how poor they were. Would-be or not, I was a serious scribe, or that is what I told myself; at any rate, I considered myself a poet and therefore owned that expensive black spring binder into which I gathered my latest poems, along with the ones that had passed muster and would be included in my first poetry collection whenever publishers came to their senses and wanted to print my work. At least that was the reasoning behind whatever compelled me to purchase an expensive bit of office equipment.

My only other expenses were cigarettes, which I rolled myself, and taking buses to and from work. I paid my rent to an old Ukrainian landlord who had a hardware store on Avenue A, right across from Tompkins Square Park. Whatever moneys were left I would buy books, new and used, at the Eighth Street Bookshop across town in the Village or in those great old booksellers on Fourth Avenue or from that old man in the tiny bookshop on West 4th Street where I had purchased the spring binder.

I had no telephone.

Oh, yes, there was also the matter of the most expensive item in my budget: the rent was sixty dollars a month.

I can't remember ever getting a utility bill.

Entertainment consisted of drinking in local bars when I had money, usually when I was paid my salary. Mostly I attended free local poetry readings downtown. Every Monday I stopped by the open reading at St. Mark's Church—not in the church proper, but in a hall in the back of the building, where the poets and others had to walk past a cemetery in which Peter Stuyvesant, the first governor of New Amsterdam, supposedly was buried. New Amsterdam was what this island in New York Harbor was called before the British arrived and renamed it, as the saying goes, New York, New York—so good, you had to say it twice.

I typed new poems from my notebooks after work at the music library; sometimes I had the audacity to type them at my desk in the library, in between waiting on patrons looking for musical scores by Mozart. If it was a Monday night, I typed some poems at home and headed over to the church a hundred paces west of my apartment. No matter how early I arrived, the poet Paul Blackburn was already there, setting up his reel-to-reel tape recorder, talking to different habitués of East Village open readings.

At one of these Monday night readings, I heard poet Carol Bergé describe fucking as the Village handshake.

Ranters and ravers were there, waiting to get up to terrorize us with their predictions and threats, their screaming, strident voices warning us of imminent doom, before someone, metaphorically speaking, got the hook and removed them from the stage. People mumbled their poems, shouted them, sang them like songs, decanted and descanted them, elongated their words, danced as they declared them to us. Someone read his poems making elaborate hand gestures that he claimed were related to ancient Sanskrit. Some read their poems so fast, the words were one big blur. A poet recited her poems based on the flags she displayed. Others read their Frank O'Hara or Robert Creeley imitations, their Charles Olson poems or their Diane di Prima imitations. Imitating Allen Ginsberg was a big thing for some Monday night poets. Sometimes the real person might be there, including Diane di Prima or Diane Wakoski, Robert Creeley or Ed Sanders, whose Peace Eye Bookstore was just eastward from the church down 10th Street, and where he also produced *Fuck You/A Magazine of the Arts*. Allen Ginsberg, bursting with creative energy, stopped by to read a new poem or something from his journal or played the harmonium as he and Peter Orlovsky chanted Buddhist verses. These better-known writers apparently came to the readings to seek out Paul Blackburn, who was universally well liked, even loved.

One poet removed her clothes, in a kind of striptease, reciting her poem until she was completely naked and then rolled around on the floor, seeming to make love to herself. She was a beautiful woman, maybe in her late thirties or early forties, her hair long, with the lithe, athletic body of a dancer. She brought poetry alive on those evenings when she showed up, full of daring energy; she flirted with the words, calling them forth. She flirted with us. She looked right at me and through me. I was in love, but it only lasted that moment, then she looked at another person in the room, and that person fell in love with her.

But life generally was more prosaic than naked dancers reciting poems as they writhed on the floor. My job at the library was to monitor the pages, among other things; the pages' job was to retrieve the musical scores which the patrons requested from the stacks. (I remember that everything by Mozart began with the call letter K, having something to do with how his music was classified.) These slips that the patrons handed my way then went to a page, who would run off at speed into the stacks to grab the music for the customer. I really do mean that they ran for the material. The pages were mostly a ragtag group of young men, in high school or working their way through one of the local universities, such as City College in Harlem, Queens College out on Long Island, or Brooklyn College in the borough where I had lived as a child.

To all outward appearances, I had a fairly dull life. My inner life was quite another matter. Footloose as a result of being turned down by the local draft board for the second time because I failed the physical, I had both an inherited and newly acquired wildness in my soul. At the draft board, my blood was dirty with drugs and alcohol, my heartbeat was irregular, and I had the general demeanor of a crazed anarchist. I had been taking pills like they were M&M's, and I had consumed copious amounts of poppy-seed bagels, working on the unscientific theory that the poppy plant was the source of opium, and it would throw off the reading of my bloodwork. Perhaps it did; after all, I had been turned down again by the military/industrial complex in the form of the local draft board, which I imagined feeding young men such as myself as fodder for the war machine in Southeast Asia.

A dropout from a state university earlier that year, I was now officially an American bohemian, not a beatnik—they came from another generation—but a hippie, with my long black unruly mop of hair, a scraggly beard, and my East Village costume, which included a pair of beat-up jeans or khakis, sneakers or work boots (depending on the season), a raggedy corduroy jacket, and cheap chambray shirts I bought from the nearby Hudson's Army & Navy store at a time when such places had reasonably priced and durable clothing.

Someone in my family showed me a photograph that a *New York Daily News* photographer had taken. The caption to the photograph said it all: *Wild-Haired Hippie Takes in Scene at Tompkins Square Park.* The photographer had snapped me in that park. I was indeed wild-haired, wild-hearted, wild-assed, unstoppable, untamable, or at least I considered myself something special.

After all, I was a poet; I considered myself one; I was as good as any of the other poets I knew. It was just a question of convincing the world—or, if not the world, a few good readers—that, poetically speaking, I had something to offer.

The day that the *Daily News* had snapped my photograph, I had been sitting on a bench in the park and talking with people I knew from the college I had dropped out of. Some of my friends drank beer from cans that were concealed in small brown bags; others defiantly smoked pot in this public place, something that would get you busted anywhere but in the East Village in 1966.

Later we wound up in an apartment on the park, and it was there that I met a young poet of great seriousness and intensity. He was not messy like we were, long-haired, Beat or hippie, but rather dressed conservatively in a Brooks Brothers button-down blue shirt, khaki trousers, and loafers. He had very grown-up thick black-rimmed eyeglasses, and a serious mustache. I would learn that he attended classes at the City College of New York uptown in Harlem, and that he was the poetry editor of *Promethean*, the college's literary magazine; he worked at *Time* magazine as an editor, and already had poetry published in places like *The Nation*. This poet looked like the oldest person in the room, and yet I would learn that he was the youngest one there. His name was Ross Feld, and he hailed from Brooklyn, but now was living uptown in Washington Heights with a bunch of other would-be poets, most of whom attended City College.

Ross suggested we meet for drinks at Max's Kansas City after work in our respective jobs. It was never in my orbit that I would be going for drinks on Park Avenue, but this was a funky part of that street just north of Union Square, a more commercial part, the polar opposite of that Park Avenue on the north side of Grand Central Station and the Pan Am Building. I had never heard of Max's.

My new friend, as part of his work remit, did exotic things like flying to Chicago with the new cover of *Time* magazine. On the other hand, I had to make sure the Mozart sheets were put back in the right order before returning them to the stacks. Though I thought myself knowledgeable about poetry–after all, I had thoroughly read and reread Donald Allen's anthology–I really was just learning about contemporary American poetry, even though I had been writing poems since I was a boy, a risky enterprise in a family living in working-class neighborhoods. I thought that I had a good understanding of what a poem was; Ross was an encyclopedia of alternative American poetry after the Second World War. There was nothing, it seemed, that Ross Feld hadn't read and didn't have an opinion about. His opinions were sound and intelligent and well thought out, backed up by his prodigious reading.

When I met him for that drink a few days later, Ross

was accompanied by his Brooklyn friend, the painter Archie Rand, a precocious teen who already had paintings in a show at the prestigious 57th Street gallery, Tibor de Nagy.

Archie was a bruiser, with a big, twisted nose that suggested he'd been in a few punch-ups. In Brooklyn parlance, he was built like a brick shithouse, stocky and with a low center of gravity. He dressed like a gangster, pressed linen pants, white loafers, sheer black socks, and a black and white shirt that resembled a *guayabera*.

Max's Kansas City was a cavernous bar dedicated to artists and writers of downtown Manhattan, and it was like no other bar I had been to before or since. It was cool and unsentimental, contemporary and hip, postmodern and ironical, all brutalist angles and contrasting grays, with no references at all to an American bar, no beer signs, no sports allusions behind the bar. This was the saloon of the future which just happened to be there in 1966. Nothing resembled it in any way in this city or any other. To begin with, the space was gigantic, the ceilings high, the room capacious. Besides paintings by Andy Warhol on the walls, there were works by Donald Judd and Dan Flavin, one minimalist, the other sculpting light as well as physical volume. Max's had a gigantic picture window in the front, and during happy hour, the staff put out chicken wings to eat. After happy hour, the space once again was inhabited with a sculpture by

John Chamberlain, either one of his crushed car fenders or other parts. At one point, Chamberlain assembled a sculpture made of foam, which customers picked at until, bit by bit, the sculpture vanished.

Mickey Ruskin was Max's owner; a denizen of the night, he was tall and thin and slightly macabre with a wing of brown hair flapping across one eye. He could be a creature from an Addams Family cartoon, but instead he was a downtown patron of artists, swapping bar tabs for works of art. He was discriminating, deciding who to let into his establishment and who to banish back to the outer boroughs or the warrens of Tenafly and Hackensack, New Jersey. He was especially discerning—even uncanny and prescient—in his tastes for art, which he often displayed in Max's. The bar was a lot of things to many different customers, but it was not an inviting place to suburbanites; nor was it an Albion for the sentimental arts, plastic and otherwise, but rather a place that challenged your assumptions the minute you entered into its enormous space, and saw the often austere art works on the walls. Warhol's Pop Art was the exception to the austerity rule.

Mickey had a bit of the *poète maudit* about him; he was the Charles Baudelaire of restaurateurs.

To be admitted into Max's was not a problem early in the evening during happy hour, as most of those customers were local creative people, including such young up-and-coming artists as the painter Dan Christensen, and the sculptors Peter Reginato and Michael Steiner. But as the evening wore on and it grew closer to midnight, Mickey got particular about who he wanted in his establishment. When midnight struck, taxicabs did not turn into pumpkins and some uptown girl lose her slipper; instead, the freaks, the weirdos, and the wealthy socialites, all part of Andy Warhol's entourage at his nearby Factory, came into Max's in drunken waves. The midnight crowd was a combination of money and ambition, art and fashion, and raised existential questions about what was art and what was life and how did these two things converge in Max's Kansas City? The happy hour crowd was more down-to-earth practical, a concatenation of writers and visual artists trying to get by, but also to try to establish a name for themselves, to be taken seriously, even while out having fun.

That summer I frequently met up with Ross and Archie, usually on a Thursday evening after our Midtown jobs ended. At some point during one of these evenings, the Black Mountain poet Joel Oppenheimer showed up at the bar. Joel was the guy who named Max's after his former friend Max Finstein, who ran off with Joel's previous wife. I will leave the reason for naming a steakhouse after a guy who ran off with your wife to the stand-up comedians, Joel's shrink, or a future biographer; I have never heard a plausible reason for the homage. The Kansas City part of the name is more plausibly explained; Oppenheimer would say that a lot of steakhouses served Kansas City–style steaks.

But Max's?

Joel and Mickey knew each other from several Lower East Side coffeehouses which Ruskin had owned and managed, including Les Deux Magots and the Tenth Street Coffeehouse, where there had been a vibrant poetry scene with readings and poets hanging out afterwards. In his short lifetime Ruskin owned several different bars and restaurants where artists and writers hung out.

But that was then and this was the here and now at Max's.

On Joel's arm was his new wife Helen, about fifteen years Joel's younger. They had recently been married, not in a church or temple or city hall, but literally at Max's, the very place named for the man who ran off with Joel's first wife.

You could not make this shit up.

Months earlier, while still enrolled at the state university in central New York, I had gone with some classmates to the Ithaca airport to pick up Oppenheimer, so he could give a reading at our college. He got off the small plane right out of central casting, a poet wearing rimless glasses, with a mop of unruly prematurely gray hair, a shearling overcoat, with a cowboy hat on his head and cowboy boots on his feet. His cheeks were pockmarked and his teeth looked rotten, and he was shaking from the flight because, as he told us in the car ride back to Cortland, he was terrified of flying. He was also—we would learn—terrified of driving in cars, among other phobias. He needed a drink and, having been informed that he drank bourbon, we produced a bottle.

Now, at Max's, there stood the heroic poet once again, half a year later, looking equally bedraggled and very cool.

"You may not remember me," I said, about to give him a song and dance about being a student at the state university where I heard him read and attended a workshop in which he critiqued my and others' poems, but he interrupted me.

"You're the guy who wrote *spicket* instead of *spigot* in his poem."

I was indeed that guy.

"I'm the world's worst speller," I said.

I thought of W. B. Yeats, who was a notoriously bad speller, and I comforted myself with that knowledge, while also conceding that Joel was not a poet who thought much about William Butler Yeats, if he thought about him at all. Joel Oppenheimer was all about the American idiom, the direct treatment of the object, and no ideas but in things. At least that is what he told us when I first met him in Upstate New York six months earlier.

Joel had a great voice, full of gravel and grit, bluesy and urban; he let out a great laugh from deep in his diaphragm. He wore a pearly gray cowboy hat, and though it was a hot summer night, had on a denim shirt and a suede vest. It was probably ninety degrees outside, though inside Max's, it was cool, the air conditioning blasting away.

Helen exemplified the image of a beautiful flower child

hippie, while her new husband Joel looked like an old prospector just back from the Klondike.

"Tell them the news," Helen said.

Joel paused dramatically.

"Everyone's second choice—me!—just was made the director of the new Poetry Project at St. Mark's Church in-the-Bowery."

"Mazel tov," Ross said.

"Yeah, mazel tov, Joel," Archie chimed in.

"You know where it is, right?" Joel asked me.

"Second and 10th," I said, "I live nearby."

Joel told us that we all should come to the writing workshop he was going to offer for free to the youth of the East Village, of which I was now a member.

"And Machine Gun," he said, which is what he called me from that point until his end twenty or so years later. "Tell a few of your friends. I don't want to be preaching to an empty room about Williams's variable foot."

"Yes, sir," I said, nearly saluting him, as if he were a reincarnation of a Civil War general, but not really sure of just what he was saying until he left and Ross explained it all.

"Williams called our language the American idiom," he said, "and he often wrote in what he called the variable foot."

"Found in his book *Paterson*," Archie interrupted his friend.

"Yes," Ross said. "Found in *Paterson*."

"Which you read, right?" Archie asked me.

"Reading," I said, taking the mangled copy out of my canvas shoulder bag. I was determined to become a practitioner of this variable foot come hell or high water.

On the way home from work one autumn evening, I found a seat on the bus, planning to read until my downtown stop. It was a few weeks after I saw Joel and Helen at Max's. I was reading Williams's *Paterson*, which I now studied with almost rabbinical seriousness. Particularly on the long bus rides going home from work, if I found a seat, I would take out the book from my shoulder bag and drill my eyes into *Paterson*'s pages, practicing my poetics as a kind of hermeneutics. (I could not write that last word *hermeneutics* without thinking of Susan Sontag, as it was reading some of her essays that I came across the word; and many years later, thinking of what she wrote about Ross Feld, that she never had the pleasure of meeting him, but that she "just admired him, intensely, from afar.") So there I was reading *Paterson*. Already I had been reading Williams's selected poems, his autobiography, and some of his stories and essays. When I was not reading William Carlos Williams, I brought along my hardcover copy of Ezra Pound's *Cantos,* or took out my tattered copy of Frank O'Hara's *Lunch Poems* which I regularly stuffed into my corduroy jacket's pocket.

But on this particular bus ride downtown, I was reading *Paterson*.

The New Directions paperback had a cover illustration of the Passaic Falls, and upon seeing that cover, a passenger on the bus exclaimed, "Oh, my God, a book about Paterson, it's the Passaic Falls on the cover!" We were probably the same age or maybe she was a year or two older, though already she appeared middle-aged. She wore a business suit, dark jacket with matching dark skirt, a white blouse, some pearls around her neck, and high heels on her no doubt tired feet. The woman asked to see the book and once she realized it was poetry, a sour look came across her face, and she handed it back to me, almost as if it were covered in a smelly, unmentionable substance. Unlike this young woman in her business suit, I was not offended by poetry; what offended me was the war in Vietnam, the treatment of Black American citizens, even in New York City; poverty offended me and the government treating poverty as if it were a crime offended me; I was offended by starving children, starving artists, starving poets (myself included). William Carlos Williams's writings in *Paterson* did not offend me at all, but rather gave me a warm feeling, a purpose, if you will, and a determination to fight such a sensibility, if it could be called that, of the offended woman on the bus.

My world was charted by the streets of downtown Manhattan, with this enforced five-day-a-week bus journey to work uptown. Otherwise, I was exclusively an inhabitant of the downtown world. I lived and drank and hung out in places like Stanley's, the Annex, Slugger

Ann's, the Orchidia, Slugs' Saloon, and the Five Spot Café. Less geographical points in the East Village, these were my spiritual and cultural connections, though some might think I'm stretching the point to call a dive like Slugger Ann's a spiritual point. Nonetheless these were marks on my own moral compass, where I developed as a person, where I grew in my being. Historically, I was living through one of the most tumultuous times in America, the assassinations of John F. Kennedy and Malcolm X already facts, the assassinations of Robert Kennedy and Martin Luther King soon to become another set of facts. As writer and editor Hettie Jones noted regarding other events in the 1960s, "These are only the facts, though, which are never the whole story."

Facts or no facts, a mood inhabited the East Village. It was called paranoia, possibly fueled by the enormous amounts of weed that people smoked. People believed in conspiracies more than anything else. Everyone knew that government money was behind the invention of the Poetry Project at the church, but no one seemed to know the real story except that it was administered through a grant at the New School for Social Research in the Village. Lyndon Johnson, a hated figure on the Lower East Side, was behind it. The more paranoid among us suggested that it was part of COINTELPRO (Counterintelligence Program), that dark arts infiltration by the FBI of American creative projects. Everyone that I knew knew about Allen Ginsberg being followed and monitored by this program. Even writers as established as Ernest Hemingway were spied on by different governmental entities; some believed that the Counterintelligence Program was what drove Hemingway to suicide in 1961, five years earlier. Others ascribed his suicide to two plane crashes in Africa, both causing head injuries to the author. Supposedly the COINTELPRO was there to identify, weed out, and eradicate radical American people and organizations, "radical American people" loosely defined as creative people such as Ernest Hemingway and Allen Ginsberg. So who really funded the Poetry Project? The short answer is the Department of Health, Education, and Welfare, an integral part of the Johnson Administration. The New School administered the grant, and the Poetry Project carried out the plan. The original grant request was made to HEW's Office of Juvenile Delinquency and Youth Development. The Poetry Project's official title was "Creative Arts for Alienated Youth." I suppose I qualified as one of those alienated youths.

Like so many others in the East Village I had a suspicious paranoia about the government's funding the writing workshops and the formal and informal readings at the church. The Lower East Side was a kind of conspiracy central, with so many of the country's goofball paranoid ideas originating on those chattering streets below 14th. We knew that the two professors from the New School had written the grant proposal with Michael Allen, the rector of the church, and they had been successful in their bid, receiving a large sum of money from Lyndon Johnson's HEW. But beyond these scant details, nothing was that forthcoming, making some people even more suspicious of the Poetry Project in this antiestablishment, antiwar, antigovernment, and anti–status quo downtown place. The conspiracies surfaced especially at the Monday night readings. Poets such as Carol Bergé were deeply opposed to Joel Oppenheimer being the director of the Poetry Project. Carol believed that Paul Blackburn was the likeliest person to be director, as he had run a series nearby at the Café Le Metro steps away from the church on Second Avenue, and then a series at the church after the poets got thrown out of the Metro after a fight there. And, of course, Paul Blackburn was the maestro with a reel-to-reel tape recorder at the Monday night open readings; he was St. Mark's Prospero.

Gradually I began to piece together how the funding took place. The grant was intended to be used in a community outreach way, targeting what people in those days called "at-risk youth"—in other words, street kids—though very quickly the Poetry Project seemed to lose sight of that primary purpose, focusing instead on the burgeoning careers of the various poets and writers affiliated with the institution. The two physical points of cultural power enjoyed by the Poetry Project were the church itself, anchoring the corner of Second Avenue and 10th Street; the other locus of creative energy was the Old

Courthouse eight blocks south on Second Avenue. The tired, grim building stood there abandoned and unused for years before this cultural project came along. Besides these great conspiracies that unfolded all around us, there were other collective murmurs that were far more interesting, such as the poetry being written at the Poetry Project, and by whom, and also how these poems would show up in the monthly mimeographed magazine called *The World*, the mag edited by Anne Waldman and her partner Lewis Warsh.

The creative energy was intensely unique, and I liked living amid its unfolding, even sometimes its unraveling. It all reminded me of something I had heard about the great trumpeter Miles Davis. The jazz composer, music philosopher and theoretician George Russell once asked Davis what his highest aims in music were. What did Miles want from the music? Davis contemplated the question the way he mulled over everything. What did he want? Miles' answer was elliptical and brilliant, just like his music.

"To learn all the changes," he said.

If downtown Manhattan in the 1960s was anything, it was all about the changes. Some of these changes had to do with the differences between modal music and chords, as the discussion between Miles Davis and George Russell indicates. Some of the changes were cultural, social, and political. Most of the changes had to do with upheavals in politics-as-usual and the shifting social patterns of a place like the Lower East Side from being a ghetto for Eastern Europeans to becoming the creative playground of postwar baby boomers, most of whom came from the more affluent suburbs of America. Prescient political pamphlets heralded these changes. Everything (music, art, poetry, dance, politics, fashions, etc.) seemed interrelated, performance-based, spontaneous, and improvisational, and all I had to do was to learn these changes as they applied to the world of poetry.

What did I want from my writing?

By autumn everything was operating, if not smoothly, then bumpily but well, meaning that the workshops were taking place and young people attended them, the formal and informal readings were taking place, and I was starting to meet other young poets and writers, some of whom—although I didn't know it at the time—would become lifelong friends. Spiritually speaking, one could even say that the Poetry Project rose out of the ashes of the poet Frank O'Hara's untimely death earlier that summer. He had been on Fire Island with friends, another drunken evening in the art and literary worlds. Cars were not allowed on the island, except for beach taxis. But O'Hara's beach taxi had broken down, so the drunken party wandered about the beach, waiting for relief from another taxi. Frank was run over by a Jeep that did not see him, and a few days later, he died. A few months later, the Poetry Project began. So there was Frank O'Hara, the biggest influence of all on St. Mark's, no longer corporeal, now a poetic spirit, who exerted a major influence upon this antiestablishment arts organization. Frank O'Hara loomed over the Poetry Project like a holy ghost, its New York Paraclete, the handsome gay Harvard-educated Irishman from Massachusetts, still vulnerable and real, even in his permanent absence from St. Mark's Church. He was the most imitated poet in *The World*, and he was also the most talked-about writer. His life was lived in this neighborhood, though he would venture uptown every day to his job at the Museum of Modern Art.

Another spiritual point at the beginning of the Poetry Project was Joel Oppenheimer's ingenious first formal Thursday night reading at the church, not with himself as the star, but rather his good friend Paul Blackburn. Bob Holman's description of Paul Blackburn is still one of the best. He says that Blackburn was "the subtle father of the Poetry Project at St. Mark's Church, the pre-spirit." Many thought the "pre-spirit" would run the poetry venue at the church, but it was the outsider, a natural underdog, the present spirit, Joel Oppenheimer, who did. Everyone's second choice had become the director of the Poetry Project.

I was not exactly anyone's first choice either. I had disappointed my family by dropping out of college earlier in the year. Now I was working a low–paying job for the New York Public Library, hardly a great career move. But at least I had my own apartment now. Most of 1966 I had been mooching off an older brother who worked as a stagehand at the new opera house at Lincoln Center. His apartment was on East 49th Street near Second Avenue. The Upper East Side bars and Rodney Dangerfield's nightclub were nearby. Uptown was never my cup of tea. I thought of it as a shallow place that judged people by their possessions and salaries or, in some cases, their inherited affluence. My brother found the place from some dancers at the Metropolitan Opera House, so the tenement was filled with dancers and supernumeraries, stagehands and lighting technicians. I enjoyed the vitality and craziness while I lived there, but there was nothing like getting my own apartment.

I also inherited Midnight, a stray cat that had wandered into my brother's apartment off the fire escape. Once I had my place, I borrowed a cat transporter and took her downtown on the bus. Midnight became my closest friend. She was more like a dog than a cat, following me around the flat when I was there. We were two strays.

Now that I had my own apartment, I only saw my brother when he was on a break from his job at the Opera House, usually spent in the Century Bar on Amsterdam Avenue, just behind Lincoln Center. He was one of my older brothers, a wild kind of person who loved to drink and carry on, the perfect kind of guy to be a stagehand at the Met. We both were products of Brooklyn and Catholic educations and poverty and our parents having sixteen children, the two of us towards the top of the litter. My brother found me too tame for his tastes.

I often saw Thelonious Monk standing outside of the Century Bar, as he lived just down the block. One time, my brother and I chatted with him, then the brother went back on his shift which was going to occupy his time late into the evening. I had just finished work. Sometimes the clerks were given free tickets to musical events at one of the venues at Lincoln Center. The evening that I ran into my brother, there were no freebies on offer, so I nodded hello and said goodbye to Thelonious Monk, who acknowledged me with a nod, subtle and cool. I had already been to countless numbers of his gigs at the Five Spot, the Village Gate, and the Village Vanguard, not to mention the concert hall at Lincoln Center. Monk was probably the coolest person I had ever met; it would be hard to be cooler than he was, so I didn't even try. What I did was to try to fold his rhythms into my writing.

I went back into the library in order to get to the other side of the arts complex, where I hopped on the Broadway local subway and got off in the Village. When I came out on Seventh Avenue, I was confronted with two different faces of the city. One of these was an old building which housed St. Vincent's hospital where my mother had been a nurse; the other, across Seventh Avenue, was the ultramodern National Maritime Union headquarters, which I was familiar with, as just a year earlier, at age nineteen, I had gotten my seamen's papers and shipped out of this very hall, later assigned to work in the first-class passenger galley, scrubbing giant copper pots with a drugged-out maniac for a partner until I was able to be reassigned to the crew mess hall galley, where I worked with the nicest fellow, an old man named Manuel who hailed from Havana. Even as I daily wrote poems in my notebook, which I seemed to fill up at least once a week, I also was typing up my notes from my sea adventures in 1965.

Whenever I walked past St. Vincent's hospital, I thought of my mother working there while she was still in her teens. She had come from a prominent Brooklyn family whose businesses included a hat factory in Soho; a partial ownership of the *Brooklyn Eagle* newspaper where Walt Whitman once worked; a haberdashery on Prince Street in the South Village; and a bail bonds service that operated out of the Tombs, an infamous prison in which Herman Melville consigned Bartleby, the scrivener who "preferred not to," and which still exists today. It was at the Tombs, bailing out a felon, that my grandfather was assaulted. He was hit on the head by a heavy object, and thereafter his memory played tricks with him until his death in the 1950s. Around the same time my grandfather lost his memory, the Great Depression came, and he also lost the twenty-seven-room house on Madison Street in Bedford-Stuyvesant, which had been in the Drew family for several generations. By going to nursing school while her older sister went off to Brooklyn College, my mother saved her family from complete ruin, even though they slipped from great prominence into being just another bunch of Americans moving from one cold water flat to another because they couldn't pay the rent.

It occurred to me that I was a part of this downward spiral that began in the 1930s, but instead of despairing, I was giddy with the possibilities and juxtapositions. On one side of Seventh Avenue I saw a hospital that was part of my mother's story of redemption for her own family; and on the other side of the street, I saw a union hall that was part of my own liberation a year earlier when I shipped out to the Mediterranean. I could not get off at this stop without thinking about my mother, and how she attempted to save her family from ruin. Here I was, a selfish writer looking for the story, if not of my life, then of the lives around me, and standing on Seventh Avenue, with her hospital on one side of the street, and my own personal liberation, out of New York, out of America, out into the world, the first place our ship stopped—Casablanca.

In Brooklyn, we lived in a classic brownstone, not the luxury of my mother's home a few blocks away, but nonetheless a solid, impressive building. I lived in that brownstone and, later, in a yellow stucco house further out on Long Island in the suburbs. My family never fit in with the suburban sensibility. We were people from a rough part of Brooklyn. But as much as I loved that brownstone, I never lived anywhere that I wished to call home until I signed that lease for the apartment on East 10th Street.

So when I got off the subway and saw the National Maritime Union headquarters and St. Vincent's hospital across from each other, I thought immediately of my mother, turning over her earnings to her once-prosperous parents; I thought of my father working at Pier 90, the channel through which everyone had to go if they wanted to get themselves and their things expedited. It was his connections that got me my seamen's papers and later a backdoor visit to the Union hall across Seventh Avenue that got me on the S.S. *Independence*, and off to places like Palma de Mallorca. Walking home in the pellucid autumnal air, I had such a great sense of optimism and my own ideals and dreams. Then I got to 10th Street, and I was home; it was my home. I was going to flourish and fly there, soaring above this wonderful downtown world. Or maybe, like Icarus, I would crash to Earth, a mere mortal. But I did not care because I was doing what I wanted to do, which was to live downtown and to write.

After a light dinner at home, I walked up the block to the church and ran into Harry Lewis, poet and bartender, telling me he was going to read a series of poems about crabs. It was good to be off work, to be downtown, and to run into a friend who wanted to read me some poems about crabs. Over Harry's shoulder, I saw Allen Ginsberg talking to Paul Blackburn.

If Frank O'Hara was the incorporeal spirit overseeing the Poetry Project, Allen Ginsberg was a more corporeal presence in our streets, shouting and singing his poems wherever people were, and ready to listen. O'Hara was intangible, more present by his absence, while Ginsberg was alive and well and there, fleshy and bony and right there, the voice of our neighborhood's politics and cultural obsessions. Allen was the Buddha with the rabbinical beard, manic and Whitmanic, dharma bum and poetry's yenta. I can't remember the first time I saw Ginsberg in the East Village, including the occasional Monday night open reading at the church. He lived several blocks east of my apartment, and was ubiquitous, the unofficial mayor of the East Village, its saint and sinner, its godfather of poetry (not crime, though certainly poet of grime).

While I was never as enamored with Ginsberg's poetry as some of my friends were, I always admired many extra-literary things about him. He was politically astute, always well ahead of everyone else on matters of great urgency to the world; he was keenly aware of social injustices; and he was a born teacher, constantly evolving a poetics. When Allen Ginsberg said, "The question is how to figure out where to break the line," I paid attention.

With all this work and running around, I caught a cold. Then, my cold turned into something more serious (bronchitis), and I stopped by a free clinic in the Village. The doctor wrote me a prescription for some antibiotics. Back home, sick as a mangy dog, I remembered that there was a pharmacy at the junction of Second Avenue and St. Marks Place, so I walked the two and a half blocks from my apartment to the store, entered, and queued up, waiting to give the pharmacist the script. An old Jewish couple stood in front of me, and as they waited, they talked, not in Russian or Polish or Ukrainian, but the heavily accented English of the Lower East Side. Amazingly, they were talking about the Marc Chagall paintings in front of the Metropolitan Opera House, which I saw every day of the week when I headed towards the library. I had learned from Archie Rand that they were not tapestries, as I had thought them, but long, thin paintings. They were typical Chagall works, filled with bright colors and imaginary beings floating in the air. The old Lower East Siders went on talking about the Chagall works, and I couldn't help but eavesdrop.

"What's the big deal?" the old woman asked. "What's so great about this Chagall?"

"He's Jewish," the man said, "and he comes from the Old World."

"So does the butcher," she answered, "but I never heard anyone call him a genius."

"It's theological," the old man said.

"What's theological?"

"Chagall," he said.

"Wha!" she shouted, like a seagull calling out.

"Before Chagall," the man told her, "all angels had vings in paintings. But Chagall made angels fly even if they didn't have vings and are not angels even."

"No," the old woman said. "I had no idea that it was all

because of no vings."

"No vings," the man said.

I was feeling better, and it was a balmy autumn evening after work, so instead of taking the bus or the subway downtown, I decided to walk to Max's. It was a Thursday evening, the work week almost ended. I had found a simple way to get downtown, which was to walk down Broadway. When I got to the bar, Ross and Archie were already there, sitting in one of the front booths across from the bar. They were discussing public art. They were talking about Mickey Ruskin's collection at Max's. I got a beer and sat down. Archie asked me what art I was looking at and thinking about lately. I told him Henry Moore, Alexander Calder, and Marc Chagall.

"Why them?" he asked.

"I see them every day when I go to work," I said. "They are right outside the music library at Lincoln Center."

Harry from the Monday night open reading was there, and he came over to say hello. He and Ross were not buddies, but they tolerated each other to say hello or tell the other of a poem they admired.

Some of the regulars at the bar included Fielding "Fee" Dawson, a writer and visual artist, a Black Mountain College alum, with a halo of straight shoulder-length white hair, wearing a spotlessly clean pair of sneakers, khakis, white shirt, and tan raincoat, laughing with abandon at the end of the bar, his head thrown back and a gleam in his eye. Crazy, I thought, but very interesting. And: I probably should read him.

"Read his forthcoming book on Franz Kline, Mike," Ross said.

Archie concurred.

"It's fucking brilliant."

Fee was talking with Joe Early, a poet who, along with Ross, worked at *Time*. Next to Joe stood Donald Phelps, an expert on film and cartoons, among other things, and the editor of a very good Brooklyn literary magazine called *For Now*. Donald wore a suit and white shirt, a bow tie and a wool tweed Scally cap; he had the most excruciating stutter, which he used to emphasize his points, abandoning it the drunker he got, though sometimes the stutter grew more pronounced in drunkenness. Seeing him I thought of Humphrey Pennyworth, this huge character in the comic strip *Joe Palooka*, who drove a tiny trailer, which he pedaled. I imagined Phelps pulling up to Max's in such a contraption. He could discourse on Preston Sturges, Manny Farber, or Minnie Mouse's bloomers, sometimes all at once, sometimes one after the other in a verbal triptych.

I could not help but notice that Max's, during happy hour, was a man-cave of the arts. Over time I would see Janice Joplin drinking at the bar or Joan Baez having a tea and talking with some friends and her sister. But for the most part it was a male bastion, at least during happy hour, while the Poetry Project was more liberated. Anne

Waldman flourished; Bernadette Mayer flourished. Soon enough Alice Notley would flourish too.

Here among the guys, we ate *chic peas*, as they were called in Max's, by the handful, munched the free chicken wings, and drank copious amounts of beer. I had to go to work the next day, but then so did Ross. Fielding and Joe also had to work. But that didn't seem to stop anyone from drinking and carrying on late into the night. I knew it was around midnight when people from the Factory began to show up in groups of three to five, packing themselves into the nearby tables. Andy Warhol's crew had lots of women—socialites, drag queens, and budding starlets who worked tirelessly in his films. There were male hustlers and lots of gay men, creating a mosaic of feminine energy that neutralized the swell of the young male artists and writers who had lingered from the happy hour. 'Round midnight, the poets seemed odd and out of place among this different set of oddities and insider outcasts. For the most part we headed towards the exits. I went home to write in my journal and to type up stories and poems. I fell asleep reading *Lunch Poems*.

II.

THE EPHUS

tenderly as a
barber trimming
it off i
sing my songs, like
a barber stropping
a razor, i rage.

—Joel Oppenheimer
  ("For the Barbers")

THE EPHUS

The Poetry Project's writing workshops were free and took place on weekday evenings at the Old Courthouse. The long-abandoned building now came alive with poets in some rooms, performers and theatre artists in others, and rock musicians rehearsing, such as the young playwright Sam Shepard and his band. Sometimes the Bread and Puppet Theatre built their puppets there. Sometimes the Angry Arts poets painted their protest signs in some of the courthouse rooms. The building's neighbors included the Hell's Angels motorcycle gang one block north and the Catholic Worker, including that very human saint Dorothy Day, one block south on East 1st Street. To the west, the Bowery still functioned as New York City's skid row, the wide street lined with single-room-occupancy (SRO) hotels and beer-and-wine dives with names like the Whale's Inn at street level. Next to the courthouse, A.C. Bhaktivedanta Swami Prabhupada would shortly start Hare Krishna (Krishna Consciousness) from a storefront on Second Avenue. His followers were friends of Allen Ginsberg and street people who came in for a laugh or wanted something to eat. In contrast to Prabhupada, Dorothy Day ran the Catholic Worker, a radical Christian movement that began in the Depression era and later evolved into a pre-eminent, nonviolent, war-resisting organization. Most of the people who wandered into the Catholic Worker were winos from the Bowery or young, educated draft resisters looking for solace and advice.

That first night of the workshop, Joel Oppenheimer was late. His two assistants, Anne Waldman and Joel Sloman, nervously awaited his arrival. Sloman seemed withdrawn and, though friendly, also distant, and I later learned from some people in the class that he had already published a book of poetry with Norton entitled *Virgil's Machines*. He was prematurely bald and preternaturally quiet and withdrawn, while Waldman was talkative and vivacious. Anne had grown up in the Village and had recently attended classes at Bennington and seemed more worldly and sophisticated than all of us combined. Like other people on St. Marks Place, Anne wore a fashionable version of gypsy clothing, including a headband and peasant blouse with high boots that made her look as if she had just arrived from a dress rehearsal of Chekhov's *Uncle Vanya* or a cover shoot for *Vogue* magazine. Already I could see that half the room—myself included—had decided that Anne was our muse; I don't think she would have been flattered to learn this detail. She was friendly but also tough and, like all muses, not too tolerant of our silly notions about love and grace and the zeitgeist and the poem itself. I have never thought of Anne Waldman as a sentimental person or a sentimental poet.

"Welcome, welcome," Anne said. "Joel should be here at any moment."

Someone pointed out that Joel was already here,

nodding towards Joel Sloman.

"Our fearless leader, Joel Oppenheimer," Anne said, smiling, but steely in her gaze.

There was a feeling of anarchy in the room, bursting with nearly twenty people in attendance, almost all of them young men. The room was painted a pale institutional green; the last time it was painted was probably after the Second World War. Time had stopped in this room, and now was being rewound by our energized presence. Being the Old Courthouse, this was probably some judge's chambers. In a fine sense of poetic justice, instead of lawyers and judges, it was now filled up with poets and would-be poets, anarchists and draft dodgers, as well as people out on bail or having just skipped out on a court appearance. This old court would be our new hangout and headquarters for the poetry we intended to write. Poetry was serious business, and we were its vanguard. At least this is what we believed that first night in the Old Courthouse.

Anne, it seemed, wanted to create some order; the wild-eyed, wild-haired youth with a few exceptions, such as Ross Feld, wanted to kick out the jambs.

Before things got out of hand, Joel Oppenheimer walked into the room, and though it was still earliest autumn, he already was wearing his shearling coat, his pearly white cowboy hat, and immediately the room began to change, not only its spirit, but also its odor. Upon his arrival, the room smelt of strong French cigarettes, whiskey, and beer. His hands trembled as he sat at the head of the table, thanking Anne and Joel S. for holding the fort as he searched for a taxicab to take him from Sheridan Square in the Village to this redoubt east of the Bowery. He took out a pint bottle of bourbon, poured himself a glassful. (Yes, he had a glass at hand.) He lit a Gauloises cigarette.

Half the people in the room smoked, and there were coffee cans that people used to flick their long poetic ashes or snuff out their butts. There was even a slight trace of marijuana in the air, although it could be the result of someone's clothing saturated with its smoke before coming to the workshop.

"Have you met Anne and Joel?" Oppenheimer asked.

"I already know Joel," Robert David Cohen said.

Robert had already published poems in *The New Yorker* and *The Nation* and some other magazines. He was confident and smiling.

"Anne just got back from Bennington, right?" Joel asked her.

"It was a while ago," she said.

"These are my assistants," Joel O. told us. "When I can't be here, they will run the workshops. Both are very fine poets."

We nodded our heads in approval, almost the way people, to be cool, nodded their heads in a jazz club downtown.

Oppenheimer asked if anyone had poems to read.

A bunch of students said yes or raised their hands.

He picked four or five people, and explained that we would see how things went from that point onwards. There was no pedagogical plan, in other words, and our teacher had already said, right after he sat down, that he was an anarchist and did not particularly like rules or order.

One of the last people to read in that first tranche was a guy named Jerry. He was decidedly different looking than the others in the room. He wore a sharkskin suit, kind of like one I had seen Thelonious Monk wear. He also wore a dress shirt and tie, both of them black. He had rings on his fingers, an expensive watch on his left wrist. He sported a pencil mustache, and I almost felt, upon first seeing him, that he was in the wrong place. He was not earnest like the rest of us, but rather street-savvy and cynical and tough. Well, street, if not tough. Soaking wet he could not have been more than a hundred and twenty pounds. I thought maybe he was a Mafia guy from Little Italy, several minutes' south as the crow flies.

After Jerry read his poem, Joel Oppenheimer asked someone to pass the poem forward so that he could read it on the page. "You're Jerry Greenberg?" "Yeah," Jerry said, "that's who I am, at least today." "Greenberg," Oppenheimer said, "this is fucking fantastic, where have you been all my life?"

"I was advancing my habit one spoonful at a time," Jerry answered enigmatically.

My friend Ron Edson turned to me and shook his head

as if to say, It takes all kinds to make a village, even in the Village or, in this case, the East Village.

"It's a fucking good poem," Joel said, repeating his first instance of praise.

"I work in publishing," Jerry answered, "and I also worked in a print shop."

Joel lit up.

"I worked in a print shop until twenty minutes ago," Oppenheimer said.

"I know," Jerry answered. "That's why I'm here. I have a manuscript of much better poems. But this is what I had on hand this evening."

"Where do you work in publishing?"

"Porn," Greenberg said. "It's a schmatta in Times Square."

Schmatta: a rag.

Some of the others who read work that evening were Robert David Cohen and Brad Stark. Both read sophisticated poems, and Joel Oppenheimer praised them for their deft way of writing, even though, as he said, "It is not my way of doing it." Anne said the poems were too formal for her taste, and Joel Sloman talked about how complex the ideas were in both writers' poems. After the workshop, many of us went to the ROK bar to continue the conversation. Ron and I walked up Second Avenue with Ross and Robert, who were friends, but also seemed to have a tension between them. They heatedly argued with each other about the Objectivist poet George Oppen, who had been a communist, then seemed to disappear from poetry for several decades, but was back publishing his poetry with New Directions. Robert admired the poems; Ross was furious about them for another reason, which was Lower East Side politics. Robert was left-wing. Ross was not; he was conservative, with a capital C. The tension, though, was not within Robert; it was Ross's tensions with just about all the politics of the East Village at that time. Ross's politics were really the conservative ones of my relatives in Flatbush, not far from where he grew up.

We arrived at the bar, but Robert went on his way. So did most of the others. Ross and I and Ron and some others went into the ROK.

tho the song be
pure as anything, if
the mode be not right,
if the mode
be not pure

My life was not all poetry. I still had to get up and go to work five days a week. I walked around the East Village, vulnerable as anyone else to the crazies on St Marks Place or going down Second Avenue, being hassled by street kids (gangs of them) for having long hair and a beard and dressing so differently than they did. Through all of these stresses and strains, tensions and adjustments,

I decided to have a party, inviting several people from Lincoln Center down to the East Village. BYOB. Or pot or whatever. About twenty people showed up, including a sister closest to me in age. Kaitlin decided to bring a few of her friends, and she particularly wanted me to meet her friend Diane, who was a painting student at the School of Visual Arts on 23rd Street, less than a mile away. Diane was a great practitioner of the art of silence, something I aspired to, but had not yet mastered. Words, for me, were like the stars, shining brightly, out in the universe. I loved words. She did not, or at least, she did not seem to care for them. I thought of Beckett immediately, whose silences were a kind of philosophical and comical utterance, the language of silence. Diane's silence was neither comical nor philosophical. Her language did not deal with words but images; her painting was how she expressed herself. But we seemed to hit it off, and after the party, she came by and painted in the front room—she liked the light—and we hung out. She was not interested in beer or wine or pot or hash or any of the cultish things that East Villagers were hung up on, including reading Herman Hesse's *Siddhartha*, listening to Bob Dylan's or The Doors' records, or demonstrating against the war. She never moved in, and yet she was often there in the flat, painting in the front room. I would cook a meal of lentils with brown rice, and we would eat at the tiny table in the kitchen, not talking. I would try to get her to talk, but she didn't seem interested in it, though she was pleasant enough, smiling and sweet, spending the night on the mattress on the floor of the front room.

Naked, Diane was a kind of goddess, her figure so statuesque. I imagined her as Diana, the huntress. Diane, the human, no goddess really, mute and mysterious as Cassandra, the Cassandra of Aeschylus' play *Oresteia*, in which she no longer speaks. Diane the human came and went, showing up on my doorstep, spending the night. By morning she was gone, even before I was up—usually quite early—to get uptown for my job at the library. Sometimes she went home to Long Island; sometimes she stayed with her art school friends. At other times, she stopped by my place, never planned, never discussed, though maybe intuited.

She must be coming tonight, I would think, I had better get home early and make some lentils or beans, the smell of onions and garlic in the hallway leading her to my place on the fourth floor.

My lack of a telephone made reaching me almost impossible, and yet through some kind of extrasensory perception, we managed to meet up somewhat regularly. I would be walking down 10th Street from Second Avenue; she rounded the corner at First Avenue. We waved. Embraced. Went upstairs.

We kissed hello, nothing extravagant.

Sex occurred in the night, sleeping then waking, then going at it, then sleeping again. Naked, it was still hard to see her as anything other than the goddess.

To say that Diane and I did not know each other is understatement.

We were clueless, yet compatible, intimate at times, though mostly distant, friends to be sure, but what else?

She always wore paint-splattered jeans and sneakers, even in winter.

She had an autumn-like leather jacket that she wore.

Jacket off, she had on a paint-smeared tee-shirt, her dirty blond hair looking uncombed, or maybe she just put her fingers through it. Her fingernails were dirty from painting.

It was not exactly love, but it wasn't bad, whatever it was.

I had this feeling that she would find her soulmate on Long Island, in the suburbs, among the people most of us were fleeing. And yet, when she painted, she became transformative and unusual, not just another suburban girl in the East Village. There was a kind of spirit that she inhabited when she painted. I am saying "transformative," but what I really mean is that Diane was transcendent when she became "the painter," when she moved in the vocabulary of the visual, her silences became suffused with the energy of art, a power that put me in awe of her talents.

There was a 3' x 2' painting that she had been working on, the leaves on the trees in the background so detailed, the motorcycle in the foreground flawlessly executed. She painted in that style which became known as superrealism. It was done in oil paint, so she would leave it for a few days, disappearing once again, coming back when the paint dried, setting up her painting equipment in the front room. The brushes. The tubes of paint. The linseed oil. The empty cans in which she mixed her colors. Even though she was a realistic painter, Diane's personality was more ethereal, not quite of the Earth.

"The light, the light," she said, breaking the silence.

When I write that not everything was poetry, I am lying or delusional. I often woke in a reverie, thankful to be alive, to have my own apartment, to be working and earning a living, however humble it was, and always writing in my notebooks, filling literally hundreds of them during the time I lived in that apartment. Then there was the sensuality of poetry, of poets, and even of poetics. Poetry was its own kind of turn-on, a life energy, a force of nature, not a profession or even a calling, but simply a way of life—dare I say it, a lifestyle. No, a lifestyle is what the rich had. I had a way of living in the world. I had some peace in the midst of war; I had my own sense of beauty and truth, or maybe it was this handsome rotation around the circadian rhythms of New York City. If not the truth, it was a world of facts, such as a poem "working," a line "declaring itself," a word or even just a syllable standing up to a world of bullies and creeps.

There was something beautiful to these ugly streets, and there was no denying that many of the young people

I met were full of that radiance and beauty.

Some of the East Village's poets were as alluring as movie stars. But not Joel Oppenheimer. Joel was down-to-earth, salt-of-the-earth. One of his poems is about the pock marks on his face, comparing himself to a Surinam toad. (You can't get more funky than that!) He talked sex, but there was a celibacy in these Poetry Project rooms where the workshops met, and where the monkish work of writing poetry took place in the agora of the Poetry Project. But then these isolators and introverts assembled weekly in the workshop, sharing their poems, taking or leaving the advice of our teacher and our classmates. When I try to picture Joel, I often think of this description by Hettie Jones in her memoir *How I Became Hettie Jones*. She describes him as "bearded and bespectacled and wild-eyed as a young Trotsky, who approached her [Billie Holiday] while the rest of us kept a respectful distance. In the darkness the turned-up collar of his black overcoat seemed all of a piece with his hair and beard, and he must have been a sight to Billie."

Politically and culturally, Joel was a leftist-anarchist-pacifist type that was typical of the Lower East Side, where he had mostly lived since leaving Black Mountain College in the 1950s. Joel was a person of many interests, and his leftward-leaning politics were just such an example, juxtaposed, as it was, with his bourgeois aspirations. He also had an obsession with the American Civil War, games in general (war games in particular), working-class bars and saloons, baseball, and Marilyn Monroe. In 1966, though the titular head of an arts organization dedicated to the promotion of the arts to enhance the well-being of at-risk street kids (myself among them), he seemed to prefer the company of the hacks and flacks, the two-bit journalists and the one-bit politicians in the West Village.

Joel was friends with a lot of Irish American journalists like Pete Hamill and Joe Flaherty, men who sat at the bar listening to his bullshit hour after hour. The *Village Voice* newspaper was then located on the pie-slice-shaped corner with Seventh Avenue and Christopher Street next to the Lion's Head. Newspaperwomen and -men from the *New York Times,* the *Daily News*, and the *New York Post*, as well as from next door at the *Voice* came to drink at the Lion's Head. "But it was not just a newspaperman's bar," Pete Hamill notes in his book, *Downtown: My Manhattan*: "There were stockbrokers in the crowd, and off-duty cops and firemen, and ballplayers, and old communists, and folksingers, seamen, priests, and nuns."

Of his friend the poet, Hamill wrote: "I loved talking to Joel Oppenheimer, about baseball and politics and the art of typesetting."

Besides the writers, there were others at the Lion's Head worth noting, such as the actor Jessica Lange, who was the waitress in the backroom. In the kitchen, the poet Tom Weatherly was an assistant to the chef. One of the owners was Al Koblin, who could handle any of the egos at the bar and who often observed that he was one of the few people in the bar with a formal education and a college degree. The bartenders ranged from a male model to a sea captain and a weekend yachtsman. The great blues folksinger and legendary guitar player Dave Van Ronk trembled in the backroom with the shakes; the Irish folksinger and squeeze-box artist Joe Heaney sang there late at night; the character actor and model Frank Harris, who looked like Wild Bill Hickok, and who had the same birthday as my own—March 4th, the only full sentence in the calendar (as we erroneously liked to say)—was also present at the bar or sitting in the backroom. Joel Oppenheimer was most at home in this Village circus that was fueled by alcohol and male bullshit and was a throwback to another time when being a bohemian had a genteel nuance to its circumstance.

Like many an alcoholic before and since, Joel lived by his fears (false evidence appearing real) and his compulsions (to drink the moment he got up) and his obsessions (for booze, talking about women, hanging out with sports-writing men, small talk, idle company, and a well-prescribed routine, including how he got to and from locations like the Lion's Head). There was always a lot of romance surrounding this bar and Joel Oppenheimer's association with it. But the truth was less colorful and sentimental. Oppenheimer was drinking himself to death, not like Jerry Greenberg, who said he was dying one spoonful of dope at a time, but rather one shot/one glass of a beer at a time.

Back in the East Village Paul Blackburn walked around sporting a large black cowboy hat, drinking two-fistedly of the ales in McSorley's on East 7th Street or glugging from a bottle of Fundador brandy at the doorstep to St. Mark's Church, as if he were one of the Bowery's bums, which he certainly wasn't. Paul Blackburn had as refined a literary temperament and point of view as anyone downtown, around town, across the country, and in the world; he knew many languages, and was one of the few admirers of Ezra Pound who had actually met and conferred with the old man. I once heard Blackburn, before a Monday night open reading session, describe a meeting with Pound in Rapallo. Before he could gain access to the master, Olga Rudge, Pound's companion, demanded that Blackburn recite something that Pound had written. Paul rattled off an entire canto by Pound, then spent time reciting his own Provençal translations to the man whom T. S. Eliot called "*il miglior fabbro*," which could roughly be translated as "the finer craftsman" and which is an allusion to Dante.

By contrast, in the Village, Joel Oppenheimer, the journalists' poet, the drunk's drunk, wore a large white cowboy hat to Paul Blackburn's black one. Cowboys were everywhere downtown, from gay bars in the Village where Western kit was a male type, to the poetry and off-off-Broadway theater scenes, where the young Sam Shepard filled his plays with cowboys and ideas about the myth of the Old West.

I saw this penchant for cowboy kit as going back to one's American childhood, playing cowboys and Indians, and how American boys invariably wore cowboy outfits, whether they were gay or straight. There was a kind of extended childhood being enacted in the alternative American poetry world—particularly in the East Village where people's childhoods, though they may have been unhappy, nonetheless were certainly long, usually well into adulthood and approaching middle age. In the 1960s in downtown Manhattan, it was never too late to have a happy childhood.

Joel carried the idea of the West beyond his dress, though. His single foray into stage drama was a one-act play performed at the Judson Church's poet's theater entitled *The Great American Desert* (1966), a play about cowboys and the dreck of the modern age. Cowboys come and go in Oppenheimer's poetry, though certainly nowhere near as much as they appear in Sam Shepard's plays or in the poetry of Ed Dorn, author of *Gunslinger* (1970), a multi-volume poetic saga of the Old West. (Dorn was one of Oppenheimer's classmates at Black Mountain College.)

the calculation of
a barber is immeasurable,
the cunning, the sly
skittering about the
head

Besides Donald Allen's anthology of poetry from Grove Press, there was another collection of alternative verse that everyone I knew seemed to own and read regularly. It was called *A Controversy of Poets* (1965), edited by Paris Leary and Robert Kelly. Reading these books, I learned, from Joel's different biographical notes that he was born in the 1930s and raised in Yonkers, New York, just north of the Bronx. I learned that he had studied at Cornell University and the University of Chicago, where he majored in engineering, but never completed his studies. He wound up at Black Mountain College, an institution that he would forever be associated with, and where he met his two mentors, Charles Olson and Robert Creeley, the two figures one most thinks of when using the term "Black Mountain poets." As he proved later in the 1960s when he began to write a regular column in the *Village Voice*, he was an excellent prose writer. His two bios are, like his poetry, without any wasted words, concise and to the point. He notes that he was born during the Depression, but that he was "too young to remember any suffering." Ditto WW II. Too young, he says, but "in school and 4F during Korean." The next sentence is pure Joel Oppenheimer. He writes: "Consequently, having missed the 3 major social calamities of my time, I am always feeling just a little guilty." Joel would always be feeling just a little guilty about everything; even becoming the director of the Poetry Project made him feel guilty.

At Black Mountain College, in addition to studying poetry, Joel learned to become a printer. Thus in his Kelly/Leary anthology he states: "Believe with Williams that poetry is the most difficult of the arts, and, following his lead in another direction too, find it bugging but helpful to be working daily in another field; Olson once said I was the only man who had learned a trade I could live by at Black Mountain, and I'm only a little guilty about this fact. My verse seems concerned for the most part with the interpersonal relationship: man-to-woman, man-to-man, man-to-child; otherwise I drink, love, and play games."

In both biographies, Oppenheimer notes that he is "a little guilty," first about not serving in any of America's major wars but also not remembering America's economic and social collapse during the Great Depression of the 1930s, when he was a boy. Oppenheimer is a little guilty about learning a trade at Black Mountain College while all his classmates studied the purely theoretical realms of poetry, painting, and dance. Like the old intellectual Jews who preceded him, Joel Oppenheimer needed a line of work to pay the bills if he were going to be a poet. Perhaps it was Joel's Jewish practicalities that led him to William Carlos Williams, a poet but also a family doctor in suburban Rutherford, New Jersey.

A day would not go by in Joel Oppenheimer's company in which he didn't mention William Carlos Williams by name or quote from his poetry. Through Oppenheimer's prodding, I read Williams' *Autobiography*, which I most remember for the doctor's perspicacity regarding employment when he was a teenager. He wanted to be a poet, but he understood that poetry was not going to earn him a living. Therefore, he would become a doctor. The logic is so simple, yet profound. Such a simple decision requires a mature sense of the world and one's true worth within it. When I read that part of Williams' autobiography, my heart dropped into my stomach, realizing that at fifteen or sixteen years old, I should have been strategizing a professional career that would allow me to be a poet too. My teacher had had a trade; so did Joel's spiritual father William Carlos Williams.

Like the good doctor, Joel Oppenheimer saw that he needed a trade, and chose printing, a profession that went back to Gutenberg, a trade that had been around for five hundred years, and a lot earlier in places like China and Korea. Oppenheimer was virtually the only person at Black Mountain to learn a trade in addition to studying literature and poetry writing. But there again is Oppenheimer's perpetual guilt. He is "a little guilty" about learning that trade; why, he doesn't say. Guilt is not a feeling that comes and goes with Joel Oppenheimer; it is part of his human condition, as natural as breathing, and so therefore we must conclude, as natural as breath and syllable, the Olsonian units by which Joel wrote poems.

In the Kelly anthology, Oppenheimer notes what his concerns in writing are with interpersonal relationships, which puts him in company with Chekhov, Ibsen, and other great Modernist writers. He concludes by saying that "otherwise I drink, love, and play games." Well, yes. During his brief reign as director at the Poetry Project, he almost never drew a sober breath. As for love, he was now on his second marriage, and as for games, his apartment was filled with board games: Scrabble, Monopoly, war games, especially Civil War games. If you found Joel sober in a daytime Village bar, he would be playing a game, if not a board game, then a verbal one with the bartenders and the patrons, looking up statistics in baseball books, in the *Guinness Book of Records*, in the dictionary or mini-encyclopedia kept behind the bar.

Joel Oppenheimer had a seriousness of purpose as a poet, his poems seemingly loose and unstructured, although upon further examination, the writing was as tight as a pair of jeans that mistakenly got put, still damp, in the dryer. His speech rhythms were spoken, and therefore deceptive, seeming to trip off his tongue. Where was the craft? the more academic critics asked. Really, though, craft was in spades in his poems. Oppenheimer was coming out of a new American tradition of writing, and the center of all this tradition was located in Rutherford, New Jersey, in the home of William Carlos Williams. Most of the writers whom Joel chose to hang out with for most of his days and nights in the 1960s had no idea about this tradition, and so they thought of Oppenheimer as an oddity in the Village, a kind of poseur, a downtown character, but certainly not a serious one.

His rift with the poet and novelist Gilbert Sorrentino, one of his dearest friends in the late 1950s and early 1960s, had everything to do with Joel's enormous gifts being squandered at the Lion's Head, as he played the fool to the flacks, the hacks, and the creeps who thought writing like Ernest Hemingway was the only way that prose could be constellated and was literature's ultimate destination. Sorrentino saw Joel Oppenheimer frittering away that fragile gift of the lyrical poet by hanging out with sports journalists and sentimental Irish folksingers, as though Joel were afraid to face down his demons and go back to the real "community of interest" with the poets downtown. Joel avoided his old friends like Sorrentino, Fee Dawson, Joe Early, Hettie Jones, and his friends from magazines like *Yugen*, which Jones had edited with her then-husband, LeRoi.

In a parallel universe, LeRoi Jones was avoiding those old downtown literary friends, too, but for different reasons. He had changed his name to Amiri Baraka, moved uptown to Harlem, then to Newark where he grew up and where he now became a grassroots leader and activist in the Black community. Jones had rejected everything white, European, the old culture, to embrace the rebirth of Black culture that seemed to blossom like a beautiful ghetto weed in 1966 with the Black Power movement. Oppenheimer had rejected anything having to do with poetry—with the exception of his workshop at the Poetry Project which he more or less dutifully showed up to teach, although sometimes he reeled into the room, already reeking of booze, and he could not get through the couple-hour sessions without cracking open a can of beer or taking a slug from his bourbon bottle that was in his coat pocket. Personally, I loved it all, finding it theatrical and real, the essence of poetry, which I saw as being Dionysian, the embracing of the god of wine. For me, you could not do without drunkenness. In fact, nearly all the poetry I wrote during this period had to do with alcohol because Joel had said to me, "Write about what you know," and all I knew was drinking, it seemed, so that is what I wrote about, calling the manuscript "Alcohol Poems." During this period I wrote a few thousand poems about drinking and alcohol, only to throw out most and publish a tiny chapbook of them entitled *Alcohol Poems* in 1973. My poetry teacher approved. Now besides "Machine Gun," Joel also called me *emgee*, as in M.G., but lower case, as all things were for Joel Oppenheimer—lower case, he said, not because of archy and mehitabel, Don Marquis' cockroach who wrote poetry, or in a more literary context, e. e. cummings' commitment to the lower case in his poems, but because Oppenheimer was a printer.

Being a barfly was not a new job description for Joel.

As a member of the downtown alternative poetry scene that was found in the coffeehouses and jazz clubs, he hung out in the Village bars with Abstract Expressionist painters such as Franz Kline and Philip Guston in the

1950s, and he listened to the new jazz in clubs like the Five Spot Café. But Joel's favorite milieu was the local bar, including Dillons where he would spend endless hours playing board games with other patrons. He also hung out and drank in the original Cedar bar as well as several other artists' hangouts in the 1950s. But the Lion's Head was the place where most people associate Oppenheimer and his drinking. In some respects, he followed a long tradition of Village poet-drinkers, including Maxwell Bodenheim, a legendary Village character who was killed fighting over a bottle of sweet wine. "You can steal my girlfriend," he was reputed to have said, "but you can't steal my wine." (At least my oldest brother Jimmy liked to tell the story of Bodenheim that way, Jimmy being obsessed with him and determined to drink himself to death the same way. In keeping with this ambition, Jimmy often stayed in the Mills Hotel when he was in New York, a flophouse on Bleecker Street in the heart of the Village.) One forgets that Bodenheim, like Oppenheimer, was once a serious poet, for instance, Bodenheim was singled out by William Carlos Williams in his autobiography for being one of the most important poets in the early days of 1920s Modernism.

His drinking pals saw Joel as a kind of wastrel, while his old poet friends saw him as a lost cause. His endearing jitters had turned into delirium tremens. At the time, he did not yet live in Westbeth, the artists' and writers' residence facing onto the North River, but right off of

Sheridan Square in an expensive apartment. He hardly had to walk more than a few hundred steps to get from home to the bar. But even that journey had become a struggle fraught with difficulties and obstacles. He would have to say hello to people before he had a drink. He might bump into an old pal. There might be people he owed money or, worse, some old girlfriend ready to poke him in the eye (figuratively speaking) with a stick or, barring that, some unkind words, the worst blow of all.

Joel's young wife Helen—his young, *pregnant* wife Helen—was baffled, to say the least, by his behavior. Sad to say, Joel was mentally and physically going downhill at the age of thirty-six. He looked like an old man; in fact, his hair was prematurely gray, and his appearance became more slovenly by the day. I am reminded that the bebop jazz saxophonist and composer genius Charlie Parker, another brilliant alcoholic, likewise was drinking himself to death around this age, and when he succeeded, not yet in his mid-thirties, the hospital described Parker as an *elderly* Black male who apparently died of natural causes, when in fact Parker was a young man who had killed himself through drug and alcohol abuse. The sad story, for me, at least, was that I bought into the romantic idea of drinking oneself to death before forty years old. After all, Dylan Thomas, the famous Welsh poet, had managed to do it in Greenwich Village, dying only a few blocks from the Lion's Head at St. Vincent's Hospital. Joel Oppenheimer had bought into this myth wholeheartedly.

Eventually the Oppenheimers, with their children, moved to the newly opened Westbeth apartments complex on the Hudson River in the extreme west of the Village, as did the Sorrentinos, all of them moving in around the same time. Initially Joel and Gil were still the best of friends, going back to the late 1950s when they hung out in places like the Five Spot Café and the old Cedar where the Abstract Expressionist painters (Kline, DeKooning, Pollock, et al.) were drinking themselves into oblivion, having punch ups, and then going home to paint remorseless masterpieces, even as their own lives became proscribed by their guilt and shame at the night before's behaviors. The poets were more than just hangers on or groupies on the art scene; they were an integral part of it in the 1950s. Frank O'Hara's poetry is filled with these associations between writers and artists, but then so are Joel Oppenheimer's poems, as well as Gilbert Sorrentino's and even LeRoi Jones' poems. Their mentors William Carlos Williams and Ezra Pound wrote, respectively, of Breughel and Gaudier-Breszka, not to mention their personal associations with all the great Modernist artists from Picasso to Duchamps.

Joel Oppenheimer, in the eyes of someone like Gilbert Sorrentino, had betrayed his god given talents, forsaking them for the easy fame and camaraderie of becoming a character in a Village dive in Sheridan Square. But it was not simply the bullshit artists in the Village bars that Sorrentino objected to. After all, he was a great talker himself, and in a poem like "The Meeting," he freely acknowledges his own penchant for bullshit. "I have always talked, too much," he admits, "and hated it in myself." So perhaps what Gil hated about himself he saw his friend Joel becoming, not so much a writer talking about writing as Joel was becoming a talker, a charmer, a character on a barstool, talking about writing, talking and talking, but doing nothing about it. How close were Gil and Joel?"

Oppenheimer had written the introduction to Sorrentino's first book of poems, *The Darkness Surrounds Us* (1960). In reading Gil's poems, Joel observed that "we/re almost back somewhere, ireland, say, fifteen hundred years ago, a poet might just possibly get the best room in the house." There are so many levels of discourse working in these relationships between downtown poets. There is that personal level of friendship, the common ground, two people who see eye-to-eye, and share a craft (poetry) and passions, living in proximity to one another. Joel does not use apostrophes. Instead prefers a slash, making the physical appearance of his prose stand out stylistically.

Gilbert Sorrentino, on the other hand, a Brooklyn native, was the childhood friend of Hubert "Cubby" Selby, future great American novelist, author of *Last Exit to Brooklyn* (1964) and other masterpieces of American prose. Like Joel, Cubby's prose used slashes for apostrophes, as well as affecting a prose style quite similar to Joel's in this introduction to Gil Sorrentino's first book of poems. Another layer of archeological sediment to sift through: Joel and Cubby were roommates in the 1950s. Perhaps their prose styles developed in the long nights of their early friendship. I once asked Cubby Selby whether he was influenced by Joel's prose style, and he said: "Mike, I was under the influence of everything from writers to painters to booze to heroin. Take your pick about influence." When I asked Oppenheimer the same question, he scratched his head, thought and said: "Which came first, the chicken or the egg? I guess we both discovered the slash at the same time, and then used it." The only "roommate" situation weirder than Hubert Selby living with Joel Oppenheimer was that of Marlon Brando living with Wally Cox, Mister Peepers, also downtown in the Village. But then again downtown life brought odd bedfellows together. A Jew from Yonkers, by way of the Lower East Side and Middle Europe, becomes best friends with an Irish kid from Brooklyn whose paternal family was from Sciacca in Sicily. What do they have in common? The American language. It is the language which William Carlos Williams said came from the mouths of Polish mothers, which I presume the doctor meant was somewhere in New Jersey. Doctor Williams also said that "we poets have to talk in a language which is not English. It is the American idiom," which he also said had "as much originality as jazz." In 1967, four years after Williams had died, two of his poetry off-spring, Gilbert Sorrentino and Joel Oppenheimer, were discoursing in such an idiom, and their own personal differences were about how much respect and care was needed to preserve this gift. Joel wanted to waste it to the four winds or piss it away down the toilets of The Head, while Gil acted as its custodian, its curator, shepherding the gift ever onward into the next generation. Sorrentino, I think it fair to say, was obsessed with comic strips, especially from his Brooklyn childhood, and his own poems are filled with these characters, including Major Hoople, Moon Mullins, and Lothar, to name just a few.

Diane came by irregularly, sometimes spending a week at my flat, other times missing in action for a week or two or even a month. Around the holidays she would spend time out on Long Island with her family. Like Da Vinci traveling everywhere with the *Mona Lisa*, Diane never traveled anywhere without her super-realistic painting of the motorcycle, with its elaborately painted greenery of leaves and bushes. (But the one exception was when she left it with me, so that it could dry before she brought it with her to school or back out on Long Island.) Thus it was often under her arm, a drop cloth draped over it, as she schlepped up First Avenue to school or rounded the corner heading towards my flat.

I wrote poems; she painted. Sometimes we ate together silently.

She might smile at me. She was still beautiful and mysterious. I considered myself lucky to be with her.

She worked meticulously on the motorcycle painting. Sometimes I kidded myself and would think that she was going to give me the painting as a gift. But that was sentimental wish fulfillment, and rubbish, not a realistic assessment of the situation. She had no more intention of giving me the painting than she did of coming into the apartment one day and reciting, from memory, Yeats' poem "The Second Coming."

There was a knock at the door, which I opened without asking who it was.

It was Diane.

We said hello, embracing, kissing. Then she set up her paints, the linseed oil, and the turpentine. She was painting, humming to herself as she painted. I cooked my usual fare, some pulses, brown rice, carrots and onion, some celery. The room filled up with the aroma of the *sofrito.* I drank a beer, smoked a cigarette, and watched her as she worked. She must have sensed my male gaze, because she looked up, smiled at me, then went back to painting, as if she was in the room by herself. I lay on the mattress, reading some poems, this one a strange book called *The Heads of the Town up to the Aether* by Jack Spicer. I had never read anything quite like it. The next day she went back to Long Island after a day at the art school. I sat at home, alone, reading poems by Joel Oppenheimer and Gilbert Sorrentino. Already I was aware that there was a division with their friendship.

In the late Fifties and early Sixties, Oppenheimer and Sorrentino were published in magazines like *Yugen*, edited by Hettie and LeRoi Jones, and all of them hung out at the Jones' home, partying and talking about poetry and listening to jazz and discussing radical politics. Joel Oppenheimer's alienation from LeRoi Jones had nothing to do with Joel's life-style or his habits or personal obsessions. It was simply politics. In the 1960s, Black power, really Black Power, was coming into focus, a series of young Black leaders merging their energies, ideas, and political agendas into a formidable wedge in the American political psyche. For LeRoi Jones, the transformation from downtown bohemian to uptown Black leader was not overnight, nor even a slow progression throughout 1966, the year Black Power came into its own. Downtown was a kind of epicenter of this Black Power activity, especially bars like Stanley's where the jazz was live and the discussions in the corners of the room were all about radical political action. Revolution was the word of the moment, and it was not used idly, but with the intention of affecting a sea change in America. LeRoi Jones—soon to become Amiri Baraka—would shortly turn his back on his esthete friends, the white poets and artists of his youth, and make his way towards Newark, his childhood home, and become a prominent African American leader, not just in the local community or within the poetry scene, but throughout the country and even the world. It is impossible to know where Baraka's radicalization begins, but he had to endure things that his white friends did not. Even in Frank O'Hara's elegantly rendered version of New York City, found in *Lunch Poems* (1964), untoward things happen to Black men in 1950s America. In O'Hara's "Personal Poem," he writes about being uptown at Moriarty's, a swanky uptown East Side bar, waiting for Jones to show. When he finally shows up, he tells O'Hara about Miles Davis being clubbed twelve times by a cop in front of Birdland. By 1960, LeRoi Jones was involved with Fair Play for Cuba, and in July of that year, he went with a delegation to Havana to celebrate the seventh anniversary of the Communist Revolution in Cuba by Fidel Castro. It is where Jones was reputed to have found politics. Jones' other medium was of course poetry, something he did exceedingly well, becoming one of the top poets downtown. His poetry was known internationally; even Fidel Castro knew that LeRoi Jones was a prominent alternative downtown New York African American poet of some renown. After all, he was, along with several other Black intellectuals, a guest of the Cuban nation, taking a place of honor on the dais with Fidel Castro. Not only was he an important poet, Jones' home in the East Village was where everyone regularly gathered to talk and hang out.

Joel, Cubby, Gil, and the other downtown writers (nearly all of them white), were close to LeRoi Jones for a variety of reasons. They admired LeRoi's writing, both his poetry and prose and his now burgeoning playwriting career, as well as his acumen for editing and anthologizing, his speechifying and testifying. I first encountered Jones, not as a poet, but as a playwright—a very powerful one at that—and as an essayist, as he wrote what for me was one of the best essays I had encountered in the 1960s, about his visit to Cuba, publishing it in an issue of *Evergreen Review*. Downtown, Jones' friends admired his moral and political character, or they simply liked him as a friend, a dear friend, someone who shared a common vocabulary (out of Williams, Olson, Creeley, and others) with them. Jones jettisoned these friendships, not disowning so much as simply moving on from them. This political action at the grass roots level of the downtown world disturbed everyone, Joel Oppenheimer included or, I should say, particularly Joel. He often spoke of the loss of LeRoi Jones' company with great forlornness, hang-dog sad. Losing his friendship with Jones, I imagined at the time, was one of the great losses of Joel Oppenheimer's life, far worse certainly than his friend Max Finstein running off with Joel's first wife.

As his poetry eminently made clear, Joel had trouble with women, so that the loss of a female companion was part of what he expected from life. He did not expect his dear old friends Gil and Roi to abandon him. They were his stalwarts. The greatest times were had in bars with these people. Now they wanted nothing to do with Joel, whom they thought of as an embarrassment, an anachronism, someone no longer of his time. Joel's own alcoholic haze had created a wall of fear around him, so that the 1960s were not even there. Instead, it was the 1950s all over, only late in the decade, and everyone was out drinking and misbehaving and having fun, talking a lot of trash about what they were going to do, whether it was writing a poem or a story, a play or a novel, a collage or a painting. First they were going to get shit-faced. Then they were going to go home and write or paint like it was nobody's business. In those days, Joel did go home to write his delicately lyrical poems of domesticity and living in the working world. Ten years later, deep into the night, he didn't even know his own name, much less that he was a gifted poet. He had been sitting all day talking to the journalists, not about poetry or politics, but sports, not because sport was that interesting, but because talking about sports was a way to avoid talking about life—a way to not have to deal with life at all. The fear seemed to abate when he talked about sports, if only for a moment.

But I should talk. I spent long periods talking about sports to people in the bars. I was avoiding my life, too. I had a nonverbal, physical relationship with a young woman whom I hardly knew beyond the flimsiest of details. We had sex whenever I saw her, and it was good. It was very good, as Hemingway would say. And yet our relationship lacked intimacy. Did I know her favorite color? Was it red—like her motorcycle painting—and who was her favorite painter? Did she have a favorite piece of music?

What did Diane think of me or what did I think of her? To be sure, I was a novice at relationships, unlike my poetry teacher who readily admitted his interest in interpersonal relationships and games. Diane was my first girlfriend, if indeed she was my girlfriend. I had no girlfriend in high school or college. I rarely if ever discussed my writing with Diane; no, no, I never discussed it with her. She never talked to me about her paintings or drawings. I enjoyed her company and the attention for however briefly it was as a moment of nonverbal connection, not intimacy, but something approaching it, and yet miles away.

Diane got up, stepped into her paint-splattered jeans, put on her sneakers, her bra, her paint-smeared tee-shirt, said goodbye, and went back to Long Island.

How could I critique Joel or anyone else?

He was a published poet, with renown in the downtown world.

We all aspired to writing poems like Joel's, concise, lyrical, insightful, achingly beautiful, full of objects evoking feelings, the bluesy quality, the struts and architecture of poetry, creating emotions from mere words on the page. How was that done?

Whatever one thought personally of Joel Oppenheimer, an evening spent in his company was electrifying. You could see the man disintegrating before your eyes, and yet his voice was deep and resonant, filled with the gravel and experience of an urban blues singer, and he spoke so coherently about his passion for writing. His take on poetry was not as unorthodox as some might think. He was of the tradition, if by tradition one meant Williams and Pound, Olson and Creeley. But it was a proscribed poetics, even to acolytes like myself. If you drifted beyond the precincts of Black Mountain, Joel could be as severe as the Franciscan monks of my childhood, whapping your knuckles (metaphorically speaking in Joel's case) with the wooden triangular ruler. Joel Oppenheimer did not fancy us writing like Frank O'Hara or Ted Berrigan, though he might compliment us for writing like Paul Blackburn or Ed Dorn. He was far too vulnerable to be truly macho, and yet some of the things he said could be construed as being macho, certainly words that were not sensitive to what Frank O'Hara called "feminine, marvelous, tough," though Joel might sanction the last type of poem—a tough one—he didn't seem at all inclined to see us write either the feminine or marvelous poem, not even the women in our workshop class, many of whom were marvelous and tough. Certainly Anne Waldman was feminine, marvelous and tough, as were several of the women in regular attendance of the workshop, the only way they could survive in such a masculine atmosphere.

My psychological sense of other people was poor. I did not have an inbred shit-detector. When I wrote about Diane, I realize that the person who did not know how to communicate was probably me, not her. I was mostly lost in the interstices of my own mind, its peaks and valleys.

I liked weird people, strange people, outsiders, including tramps and Bowery bums and other kinds of street people. Every day I had encounters with people out on the street. It was the nature of this community that everything seemed to take place on the street. It is what I found most attractive of my new home. The street was everything. Sometimes these people of the street would venture into Joel Oppenheimer's workshop. But for the most part there was a hardcore of young men, who regularly attended his classes, and these were fairly normal, regular people, not particularly weird or different from anyone else. What we had in common, what was our common ground, was poetry, a particular kind, though, this alternative 1960s version of the outsider poem, and that was what we all searched for and tried to bring into fruition.

It would be impossible to identify every person who passed through the workshop doors at the Old Courthouse. There were no enrollment figures and people came and went as they pleased. A lot of Joel's students were also students of Paul Blackburn's at City College (CCNY), uptown in Harlem. These were the people who formed the core of the participants at the workshops. They were serious about writing poems. Their numbers included Ross Feld, Henry Weinfield, Brad Stark, Robert David Cohen, Roger Greenwald, Scott Cohen, and Elaine Schwager. As for the at-risk youths in the grant proposal from the New School, these people came and went, casually, here one class, gone for good the next. The writers mentioned above were regulars at the workshop, at least initially. Not one of them was an at-risk youth from the neighborhood.

I think that Jerry Greenberg was probably the only at-risk person regularly attending the workshops. Though hardly a youth—he was already in his mid-twenties—he was certainly youthful and risky, and very much a street guy. He was a hard-drug user, a hustler, a desperado, and an outlaw, though also a refined poet and an exceedingly well read and educated person. He was a dropout from Berkeley and his reading encompassed, not just classics of poetry, but also the edges of literary taste, including mysteries, thrillers, and pornography.

Besides his shark-skin suits, black shirts, and either black or white ties, Jerry also wore nose-picker shoes, at least that is what we called such pointy, narrow shoes in the neighborhood where I came from. When Jerry Greenberg took off his suit jacket and rolled up his sleeves, his arms were filled with tattoos, including a dragon which took up one arm. In 1966, tattoos were not as prevalent or as fashionable as they are today, so this was unusual to say the least. Only sailors and criminals had such tattoos; Jerry looked as if he had never stepped foot on a boat. Though actually from a middle-class background—he grew up in the New York suburb of New Rochelle—he seemed to be nothing but from the street. Besides his tattoos, Jerry had lots of track marks on his arms and legs, the scars of using needles for heroin. He freely admitted—though only in the past tense—that he had *had* problems with drugs, and we believed him.

I often ran into Jerry one block south of my flat because his girlfriend Sujenna lived there. She had been a stripper and a professional poker player, among other things, but now she was an elementary school teacher. She was from San Francisco, where Jerry first met her, and they had been—and would continue to be—on and off boyfriend and girlfriend for as long as I knew them. Sujenna was the first well-educated woman I had met who also had a tattoo, again, something of a rarity in 1966. Her tattoo was a butterfly on her shoulder. When Jerry was off heroin, Sujenna invited some of us over for Sunday brunch. Originally from Texas, she was a great southern cook, and spoiled everyone with her food, including homemade sourdough bread, Mexican eggs, spoon bread, jalapeño cornbread, and incredible coffee. The improvised poetry group smoked copious amounts of marijuana or my hash because in those days no one saw it as a drug or connected it to other addictions, and we'd drink beer or wine in her backyard garden, then read our poems aloud to each other. It was most civilized, to say the least.

Hanging out with Jerry was its own education in two ways: he hipped us to the various strains of music (jazz, blues, folk, rock) going down in out-of-the-way clubs and bars; and he was erudite about poetry, especially Spanish and French poetry, about which he seemed to have a doctoral knowledge. Jerry stood there reciting poetry from Apollinaire or Rimbaud, Neruda or Vallejo, out loud and from memory, at the end of which he would give his post-junkie laugh, somewhat menacingly, letting you wonder just who he was, though neither my friends nor I quite ever really knew.

At one of these Sujenna backyard get-togethers, Jerry talked to me about the French Surrealist poet Paul Eluard. He explained that an Eluard poem about a little boat was really a poem about a clitoris, and that "little boat" was a French euphemism for the female body part for sexual arousal. Being a repressed Irish Catholic, I can't tell you how grateful I was to Jerry for this information, seemingly random and useless, and yet forming the hard-wiring of my brain as it developed in my 20s. Joel Oppenheimer did not discuss such poets as Paul Eluard, Federico Garcia Lorca, Cesar Vallejo, and Pablo Neruda, probably because his own mentors–Charles Olson and Robert Creeley–did not discuss them. I was reading and hearing their poems outside of the poetry writing workshop. That was thanks to Jerry Greenberg. Jerry had already published poetry in *El corno emplumado*, a bilingual little literary magazine in Mexico that was put out by Margaret Randall. (Robert David Cohen would eventually leave the workshop, travel to Mexico where he met and fell in love with Margaret Randall, and then flee to Cuba with her, where they would spend many years together. Randall was also the mother of one of Joel's children.) Jerry Greenberg published in several other literary journals in Berkeley and San

Francisco, and he was often engaged in "delinquent activities." ("Delinquent activities" is the phrase used in the original grant proposal for the Poetry Project.) This included stealing, drug use, and other street crimes, though delinquent activities probably did not include revolutionary ideas and actions, other things Jerry also espoused. He was the perfect candidate for the sociologists at the New School whose programs were "concerned with effectively moving potentially trouble-prone youths whose interests may center around a life-style of drug use or other deviant activities, to a more creative and productive existence." The problem was that Jerry Greenberg could read Lorca in Spanish and Éluard in French, but he also knew how to pick the lock of a door and where to buy the strongest, cheapest bag of dope in the East Village. He was the closest thing to Arthur Rimbaud that I would encounter until a few years later when I met the young Jim Carroll, the truest manifestation of the Gallic poet, who in this contemporary instance stood in front of St. Mark's Church, dribbling a basketball and asking me if I had seen Ted Berrigan anywhere. My friend Elio Schneeman would be another one of these Poetry Project youths too hip, too street, and eventually too strung out to survive the ordeals of ordinary life.

When he was clean and sober, Jerry got involved with a group of us in protesting the Vietnam War. We had gotten a bunch of the writers from the workshop together to form a contingent to march in the protest that would culminate in a huge human be-in in Central Park. It was mostly a ragtag bunch of hippies and old beatniks. Jerry showed up in one of his usual outfits, in this instance a white suit and black shirt, his pointy shoes, a pencil-mustache and slicked back, greasy hair, looking more pimp than protester. Jerry had a poster which read: The Soup of Real Turtles Flows Through Our Veins. It was the same sign that Jerry produced for the Mobilization against the War, so obviously the line meant a great deal to him. Someone had asked him if the quotation came from Rimbaud. "Jack Spicer," Jerry Greenberg succinctly answered. All that day of protests and celebrations, people asked him what his sign meant, and by then he simply shrugged his shoulders, as if to say, I don't know, and walked on.

I still remember a tramp coming up to us and asking: "You have fifty thousand you can lend me?" But we were all broke, high, elated about the march, comrades, anarchist poets, self-righteous, indignant, sure of ourselves, poets all, going uptown to Central Park to protest that evil war in Vietnam.

During this period, one of my younger brothers was a student at the School for Visual Arts on 23rd Street, and he and several art-school friends had squatted an abandoned building on Canal Street near the tunnel entrance. They had rigged up electricity and heating from other buildings, and were doing their painting and sculpture in the cavernous ground-floor space. Jerry Greenberg wound up staying there for a few nights, during which period he managed to rip off a group of young thugs called the Carmine Street gang in the Village. (The Eric Roberts and Mickey Rourke film *The Pope of Greenwich Village* is loosely based on the Carmine Street gang.) After taking their money and promising to return with drugs, Jerry purchased heroin for himself. Somehow the gang found out where he was, dragged him out of my brother's studio, and beat Greenberg to a pulp on Canal Street. Soon thereafter Jerry disappeared from New York. In late 1968, Jerry Greenberg re-surfaced in San Francisco. This time he had reinvented himself as a rock 'n' roll writer. He was one of the founding staff members of *Rolling Stone*, at that time a recently started magazine, with Jann Wenner as publisher and head editor. Greenberg is rarely mentioned as one of the early influences upon this magazine, and yet he was there at its beginnings, suggesting articles, writing pieces, setting up interviews with musicians— creating the tone for what the magazine would become, a place for American culture, not just its popular music. Jerry got *Rolling Stone* to publish poetry, and I have heard it suggested by other staff members that he may have even convinced *Rolling Stone* to go to that revolutionary format of a folded tabloid-sized newspaper, with the cover photo printed on the folded back page. (This seems idiotically simple today, but no one had ever thought of such a design before *RS* magazine introduced it.) It was probably Jerry's love of Richard Brautigan's writings that first got the magazine to print the quirky North Beach poet. People who knew Richard's eccentric poems and stories loved them, but his audience was limited to a coterie of San Francisco readers, just as Joel Oppenheimer's poetry was restricted to a small group of *aficionados* downtown. Eventually, Brautigan's face—in a ten-gallon cowboy hat with his bandito mustaches and long hair—would become almost synonymous with *Rolling Stone*. He was the first alternative-culture icon that *RS* created, just as important culturally as Hunter Thompson becoming its gonzo journalist.

Besides not being mentioned in the history of *Rolling Stone* magazine, Jerry Greenberg's name is not mentioned in articles and books about the Lower East Side poetry scene. Yet no one quite filled the remit of at-risk, alienated youth as well as Jerry did. In the original grant proposal for the Poetry Project, there is one passage that seems to describe Jerry Greenberg. It says: "Of those many patterns of activity that are couched in the framework of disavowal and negativism towards the larger social structure, there are some which take the form of serious self-destruction and anti-social behavior. (For example, drug use and larceny.)" No one was more larcenous than Jerry Greenberg, yet he may also have been one of the most talented people in Joel Oppenheimer's workshop. Instead of being written about in critical studies about the early days of the Poetry Project, he died of AIDS in complete obscurity in Miami. Like his idol Arthur Rimbaud, Jerry had given up poetry years earlier. At the time of his death, he had been working as a waiter in a Cuban restaurant. Until the end, Jerry read a mystery book every day.

Around the time that Jerry Greenberg disappeared from New York, Andrei Codrescu appeared from Detroit by way of Italy, by way of Israel, by way of Romania. His real name was Andrei Perlmutter, but he chose the writerly name Codrescu, which he claimed was Tristan Tzara's real name. (Tsara's real name was Samuel or Samy Rosenstock. Andrei spoke in poetic truths, not in conventional facts.) At twenty years old, he was nothing but brilliant, full of energy and good humor, and yet another encyclopedic mind for literature and, in his case specifically, poetry and politics, poetics and history, all of it wrapped around his thick as a brick Transylvanian accent, which only seemed to get thicker the longer he stayed in America. Andrei's American idiom came out of the mouth of this Romany poet who appeared upon the doorstep of the Old Courthouse. Like Moses out of the reeds, Andrei was spontaneously born a poet at Second Avenue and 2nd Street. If there were no miracles ascribed to him, he nevertheless had his visions late at night on Avenue C. At other times his visions were around midnight, as he worked in the Eighth Street Bookshop as a night-time clerk, advising customers of what was on offer in this multi-layered bookstore in the heart of the Village between Fifth and Sixth avenues.

I still recall the first time I heard Andrei say, "far out, man," in his thick Transylvanian accent, which today is a quite familiar voice because of all of his years broadcasting on National Public Radio. In 1967, there was a kind of new music to his voice, especially as he spoke in the rhythms and patterns of the East Village vernacular, with a heavily accented Eastern European accent of the Lower East Side. It was Andrei Codrescu who filled in the gap between the indigenous and the newly arrived. It was Codrescu who added another literary and intellectual layer to the workshop experience, with his references to the Dada and Surrealist poets, names like Andre Breton and Tristan Tzara tripping off his tongue. He also vigorously defended the New York School poets against the slings and arrows of other die-hard devotees to the cause of Black Mountain poetry. Andrei was the person who got me to understand why John Ashbery was so important a poet, and in those days, he liked to recite JA's poems aloud, pronouncing the words in his traveler's accent, so that today when I re-read early Ashbery poems, I still hear them in Andrei's thick, rich early American accent. Far out, man.

Then there was our fearful leader, Joel Oppenheimer, who wrote in his poem for the barbers:

> if a needle were
> dug in the middle of
> the cranium would it
> do more damage?

Back in 1966-67, there were more men than women at these free classes offered by the church. Of the ten or fifteen people who regularly attended Joel's workshop, only two or three were women, and one of those women was Anne Waldman. She was the one who practiced, not the ABC's of Reading, Ezra Pound's how-to book about poetry, but rather Anne was practitioner of another kind of ABC's (ashtrays, brooms, and chairs); she was the person who made everything run. I don't know if this had anything to do with Joel's attitude towards women generally or if it was some deeper malady in the zeitgeist. Soon enough a raft of women's names would come to be associated with the Poetry Project, including Alice Notley, Maureen Owen, Eileen Myles, Patricia Spears Jones, and Bernadette Mayer, just to name a few. Lesser known poets who attended Joel's sessions were Harriet Eskanazi, Frances Silenzi, Esther Levenberg, and Elaine Schwager. Two older woman who came regularly to the classes were Ruth Krause, whose experimental plays were produced by the Judson Theatre in the Village, and her friend Jean Boudin, the mother of the radical fugitive Kathy Boudin. It was the Boudin's townhouse, off Fifth Avenue in the Village that had blown up as the result of it being a bomb-making factory. Kathy Boudin, who never attended the workshop, as far as I know, would be involved with an armored truck heist and a murder, eventually, many years later being caught and doing hard time. The youngest

82

poet to attend the poetry workshop was Elaine Schwager, who was sixteen years old, a protégé of Paul Blackburn's, who sent her down to Joel's workshop because he was so impressed with her writing. There were lots of creative women inhabiting these sacred spaces in downtown Manhattan, and yet as Anne has rightly pointed out on many different occasions, the Don Allen anthology, the Bible of us young writers at the Poetry Project, contained forty poets—only four of them women!

Despite the influence of Black culture on the poetry scene and Black Power's influence upon the East Village's politics, Tom Weatherly was the only Black writer in the poetry workshop. He was also one of the few people to have graduated from college and to have served in the military (U.S. Marines). Eventually he would convert to Judaism, becoming an orthodox Jew. Besides working in the kitchen of the Lion's Head, Weatherly worked for many years in the Strand bookshop, and I often saw him in the shop's basement, where I would come upon this incredibly tall, athletic-looking man wearing a skullcap, a tiny pair of reading glasses perched at the end of his nose. Over the years his hair and beard turned white, giving Weatherly the countenance of a wise old character in a fairy tale.

I am not the only one to find Weatherly's face striking. The great photographer Andrei Kertesz—famous for a photo of Washington Square Park in the snow—also snapped Weatherly walking around the Village with his young wife and child. Obviously Kertesz was drawn to something in this young poet's face; he saw the poet, even amid the camouflage of a wife and family. Along with Andrei Codrescu, Tom Weatherly was one of the first of the young writers from Joel's workshop to publish a book. Andrei's first book of poems was *License to Carry a Gun* (1970). Tom's first book was *Mau-Mau American Cantos* (also 1970). Then Weatherly's output slowed to a standstill, a strategic and esthetic reason for the reduced output. Weatherly's poems became more and more concise, to the point of becoming gnomic, almost like tiny puzzles that one had to ponder for a long time to penetrate at all. Often only a few words long, they nonetheless operated on many levels, including elaborate puns and wordplay as well as containing many aspects of words at their roots, not to mention, in later years, a multitude of languages, including German and Hebrew. Like most of the people from those days, Weatherly remained true to his roots of publishing only with small presses. Profit and/or fame were never issues in his work or his life. He was committed to being a poet, which also meant a lifetime spent working in the basement of the Strand bookshop, his beard turning white, his eyes going, his back becoming bent, though he remained inordinately tall and dedicated to making poetry and helping people to find their way in the basement of the shop.

Alabama-bred and HBCU-educated, Weatherly was

decidedly more on the side of Ezra Pound than William Carlos Williams; he learned about Pound, not from Oppenheimer, but from Joel's assistant, Sam Abrams. Weatherly remained dedicated to the writing workshop for as long as it ran. He often spoke to me and other friends (Ron Edson, Jerry Greenberg, and Esther Levenberg) about the first night he came to Joel's workshop. He listened to and read from on the page the poems that other members of the group read that evening. His were so different, he thought, and he did not fit in; he thought his own work garbage. (This is what he told me years later.) It was the second time he came to the workshop that Tom read his own poetry aloud; it was an ode about an old elm in a cemetery for the Confederate dead.

There was a dead silence.

"Oh, shit," Weatherly said. "It was so bad that no one wanted to say anything because it might hurt my feelings."

After a minute or two, Joel looked around the table and he said that he could not find anything wrong with the poem. Everyone agreed. It was not a Lower East Side poem; it was a formal Southern poem, more John Crowe Ransom than Charles Olson or Robert Creeley. But a very good poem.

Very good, we all said.

Tom Weatherly was already formed as a person and a writer when he arrived at the Poetry Project, so that Joel Oppenheimer's influence upon his writing was minimal. Weatherly was more enamored of LeRoi Jones' early poetry, anyhow, and other downtown poets from the Umbra group, which many of the better known young, downtown Black poets attended. He quickly jettisoned his formal poems about Confederate graveyards in Alabama, and began to write dense, lyrical, and impossibly short, contemporary poems about being a Black man in America, the influence more the newly politically transformed Amiri Baraka. There was another influence working on Tom Weatherly that I didn't realize at the time, but seems clear to me now, and that is Louis Zukofsky, the Objectivist poet. Tom, like LZ, could pack a lot into just a few lyrically stated words. I usually came away from the workshop, when Tom's poems were discussed, going long into the night pondering what had been said that evening.

The one thing that Weatherly took from Joel Oppenheimer and made his own was to put the blues into his poems. Joel was a master at making a poem configure itself to a blues rhythm, not twelve bars or anything like that, but the imagery, and the repetitions of words and lines, the sad, hopeless quality that somehow got uplift in the singing or reciting. Tom became a blues master in his poetry, referencing all the contemporary poets but also the history of the blues, from the Mississippi Delta over to Muscles Shoals, where the Rolling Stones and other rock groups recorded their music. As Tom's poetry became more concise, his spoken utterances became equally gnomic. More and more he came to say less and less, almost as if he were practicing Wittgenstein's dictum:

wherein one has nothing to say, therein one must remain silent.

Tom Weatherly forced everyone to hear what a Black man from Alabama really sounded like. He let you know where the blues came from, and it wasn't Brooklyn. It wasn't even the East Village or Yonkers. The blues were everywhere, but their origin was in the Deep South, where Tom had grown up. He was determined to make sure that none of us forgot that truth. For Tom, poetry was not an answer to a question he didn't know he asked. Poetry, like life, was full of questions and conundrums, Black and white, with the occasional gray.

Joel Oppenheimer's poetry workshop focused on writing poems that reflected his own sensibility, and his tastes were no more in evidence than in his one-off glossy magazine, *The Genre of Silence* (1967). The title of this magazine comes from a speech that the Ukrainian writer Isaac Babel made in 1934 to the first Writers' Congress. Babel had said that the Soviet Union had given him every right but the right to write badly. As to his own small output as a writer, Babel declared that he practiced a new literary genre. He was "the master of the genre of silence." One could understand Oppenheimer's infatuation with Babel, a Jew from Odessa who hung out with tough guys. Many of the older immigrants on the Lower East Side were from Odessa. (There was even a cheap restaurant in the East Village called Odessa that the community ate at, from time to time, especially their pirogis.) But there were other things to draw Oppenheimer to Babel. The Ukrainian wrote about gangsters and street people, and he had been a Jew in the Cossack army, something that was almost unheard of. Babel, like someone from the Bronx or Brooklyn or even Yonkers, was blunt and unflinching in what he observed, and merciless in his gory details. His stories from *Red Cavalry* exemplified his tough, lyrical prose.

Not surprisingly Isaac Babel was a big influence on Hubert Selby, Jr., the author of *Last Exit to Brooklyn*.

Oppenheimer liked to quote from Babel, drawing students' attention to the *Red Cavalry* or stories such as "Guy de Maupassant" or others from *Tales of Odessa*, especially the ones about Benya Krik, the Jewish gangster.

Perhaps my favorite line in all literature dates to this period when Joel introduced us to Isaac Babel. It was a story about Benya Krik, the Jewish gangster from Odessa. A rabbi owed Krik money, and he told the old man: "If I don't have my money, Eichbaum, you won't have your cows." Afterwards, Eichbaum's barn has gone up in flames, his beautiful daughter emerges from the flames and, of course, cold-hearted Benya Krik falls in love and marries her, erasing Eichbaum's debt. Benya Krik restores the barn and gets the rabbi some new cows.

Joel often paraphrased one of Babel's lines as follows: "Nothing so pierces the heart as a well-placed period." He would punctuate the air with his dirty printer's index finger, emphasizing the bullet-like trajectory of the punctuation mark. Sometimes Joel conflated Babel's sentence with that one of his own invention, about poetry being the answer to a question you did not know you asked. Sometimes Joel blended these two ideas into one sentence, saying that poetry was the answer to a question you did not know you asked, and then emphasizing with his dirty index finger poking through the air, that nothing so punctured the heart like a well-placed period.

Isaac Babel often reminded me of my friend Tom Weatherly. Both were intellectuals and soldiers, one a Cossack, the other a U.S. Marine. But for Tom, no grammatical mark punctured the air like a bullet. As with Isaac Babel, real bullets had flown past Tom Weatherly, not full-stops or periods metaphorically described as being like bullets. Talk about no ideas but in things, the things that Weatherly knew were like a sea change compared to the others in the workshop. While it is true what Ezra Pound said that a writer can't have too many experiences, writers such as Babel and Weatherly, being soldiers, had come close to the one exception to that rule: Death.

Every week that I attended Joel's writing workshop, I was trying to figure out where I fit into all of this conversation. Clearly I was not one of the favorite young poets, and Joel Oppenheimer was very much a poet of favorites. He loved Scott Cohen's poetry, for instance, even though Scott privately detested Black Mountain poetry, preferring the

New York School of Poets, particularly Ted Berrigan, whose workshop he eventually gravitated towards. But even Scott would admit that Joel's workshop was livelier, the conversation more energetic and passionate than in Ted's. "Berrigan is a great poet," Scott told me, "but not a great teacher the way Joel Oppenheimer, drunk or sober, is." Besides Scott Cohen, Joel liked poetry from other members of the class. Early on Jerry Greenberg had won over Joel's attention. Eventually Joel pulled away from Jerry because of his erratic behavior. Weatherly and Oppenheimer were close, at first, but then drifted apart when Tom became more interested in Ezra Pound than William Carlos Williams. But it was Joel who took Tom's first book, *Mau-Mau American Cantos* (1970), to Corinth Books, the same publisher of Joel, LeRoi, Gil, Frank, et al.

Andrei Codrescu would find acknowledgment in the workshop and also publish his first book of poems, *License to Carry a Gun* around the same time that Tom did. Ron Edson was already drifting away from poetry, thinking about travel and painting and other things, like going to Mexico and teaching in New York City and getting married. Frances and Cliff moved to Maine. Elaine Schwager later became a psychotherapist. Henry Weinfield and Roger Greenwald would become academics. Ross Feld drifted away into editing at Grove Press and publishing his first (and last) book of poems with the Jargon Society a few years later, and shortly after that, his first novel, *Years Out* (1973) was published by Knopf, with a new novel from him in at least every decade until his death from cancer when he was in his fifties.

Every once in a while Joel tried to get away from William Carlos Williams and Ezra Pound, Charles Olson and Robert Creeley, and he would discuss a Latin American poet. Such an evening came to the writing workshop in the form of a visit by Clayton Eschleman, who came to discuss his translations of Cesar Vallejo. (By 1967, Eschleman was also involved in Angry Arts, an anti-war group. With a flat-bed truck filled with poets shouting anti-war poems, Angry Arts went to places like Fifth Avenue's shopping district to recite their poems to passersby.) At other times, Joel suggested students read Nicanor Parra, another South American and, a year later, author of *Poems and Antipoems* (1968). Parra even came to the class one night, reading his poems in Spanish, with Joel reading the English translations.

One evening I went to the workshop early.

The front door was already open, and so I wandered around the building, and I came upon the playwright Sam Shepard on a break after practicing with his band, who were rehearsing in a large chamber on the ground floor. The band members milled around the courtroom, but Shepard sat in one of the holding cells.

"Isn't this cool?" he asked.

"Yeah," I said, skeptically. As I walked away, I thought, Well, I guess Sam's never been locked up.

Then I went upstairs to the room where the workshops were held. Many of the City College students were already there.

The lighting was poor, reminding of bare lightbulbs on a cord that were symbols in the cartoonish recent paintings of Philip Guston, who Ross had befriended in his journeys through the art world with his friend Archie Rand. The walls were an institutional green. A folding table, long and rectangular, with about twelve to fifteen matching chairs, inhabited the center of the room whose tiny windows faced onto East 2nd Street.

As if on cue, Joel stumbled in, reeking of bourbon, beer, cigarettes, and coffee. Joel used to tell his poetry workshop: "Be there when it happens." But he was famous for adding, "Write it down." Oppenheimer bridged these two worlds at the Poetry Project—that of the performative and of the poetic. The poets associated with the Poetry Project were nothing if not performance based, and poetics was what got us to come to Joel's workshop, week after week, to discuss and argue the value of a poem's performative values as well as its poetics.

That evening I read aloud a poem I wrote about my sometime girlfriend Diane. Although she was not one for poetry, even Dee seemed to like the poem when I read it to her. It was entitled "The Positions," and I believe I eventually published it in the late 1960s in a magazine called *Galley Sail Review*, although it may also have been published in *The World*:

Diane paints, nude, in a lotus position.
(Art is the blossom she sits before.)
The purpose is, as she paints the figure,
for me to lift her, gently, under the arms,
careful, not to disrupt the posture or angle
of the legs, & fit her before another canvas,
delicate, as the brush stroke on the petals
that add to the blossom, its fragility.

It was the only poem I read in Joel's workshop which he seemed to like. All the others were more or less dismissed as "not working."

Even with this brief success, I knew that I was not a central player in the world of the poetry workshop, no matter how I tried to insinuate myself into that dialogue. But I was there when it happened, and I did write it down. Yet the poetry workshop raised questions for me about legitimacy, my own and others, authenticity, even that community of interests which Joel wrote about in his own poetry. I wrote as much as anyone in the class, if not more, being a compulsive notebook writer all my life. But perhaps it was not poetry that was finally my métier. Perhaps I needed to find another ax to play. With that thought, I walked out of the poetry workshop, not vowing to never come back again, but pondering what to do next. I was in a quandary. I found myself searching for another form in which to express myself as a writer.

I thought of myself as a writer—I was a writer or I was nothing—only I didn't necessarily see myself as being a writer in Joel Oppenheimer's mold. I liked—even loved—the poetry that Joel put forth as the paradigms. I especially liked his own poetry, particularly the work found in his early books *The Love Bit* (1962) and *The Dutiful Son* (1957). Even my siblings liked Joel's poetry, my copy of *The Love Bit* scribbled over by my oldest brother with all the passages that he loved and recited aloud during a manic phase which landed him in Bellevue and, after a few weeks of enduring me and my oldest brother, Diane even disappeared, never to return. We even had a shouting match and, one evening, even a bit more than that. It was more than a spat. I was ashamed of myself fighting with her, but I found myself siding with my older brother, who was getting ready to go full-blown psycho at any moment. My relationship with Diane had ended at that moment when my brother showed up one morning, the chemical imbalances of his brain in full blossom, he was manic, full of panic, brilliant but, being large, slightly scary. It would take me a few days to realize that Diane had gone. Even the super-realistic motorcycle painting had vanished. Her paints and brushes were gone. Diane had erased herself from my life. Where her sensuous being had once been, she had been replaced by my rotund oldest brother deep into his mania, and I repeated to myself what Ezra Pound had said aloud: a writer can't have too many experiences. Notebook and pen in hand, now also drinking around the clock as well as smoking my opiated hashish, I took up my pen and notebook. "Be there when it happens," I heard Joel say. "Write it down."

So I began to write amid the madness of my apartment.

"Write it down," I repeated.

"What?" my brother said.

Then he shot down the stairs and I saw him running down the block, screaming as if a devil were on his trail.

After my brother left, I looked at my copy of Joel's book, *The Love Bit*, and noticed that my brother had written in most of the pages in his chicken-scrawl handwriting. I had been reading and re-reading Joel's books until the covers fell off and the saddle-stitching broke. Now my brother's treatment of the book brought it further along to its ruin. I loved that fucking book, I told myself. But this did not necessarily mean that I wanted to write poetry like Joel Oppenheimer did. What I wanted was a poetry that was broad-margined enough to encompass all the contradictions of my life. I wanted a poetry that included the voices of my childhood in East New York, my friends in the playground beside the public school across from my grandmother's house. I wanted a voice that included my childhood friends, Nevo and Henley, Charleston and the others, all Black, all street kids and children of the ghetto, just as I was, too. I heard the voices of the Italian fruit and vegetable sellers who came onto our street in their horse-drawn carts, shouting things like "Melanzane! Pomodori! Mele!" and the Mississippi Delta fellow on his horse-drawn cart who shouted great words, like "Waddee-mell-own!" or "Carr-rrotts!" or "Per-tae-tas!" I heard the voice of Henry Miller speaking in his rich, strong Brooklyn resonances. Miller lived just on the other side of Broadway in Bushwick. I heard the Italian gangsters across from our house on Marion Street near Rockaway Avenue, talking about whacks and vigs and pernts (points)!

I heard my Irish aunts and my grandmother, my aunts' shrimpy boyfriends and Cuban beaux, the aunts' Irish romany ghetto goddess speech peppered with profanities and obscenities, the vernacular of the borough, its street poetry, and the poetry I wanted to write.

oh the

professionals what we

should fear.

Sitting in the discontinuous universe of my grimy, messy flat, Joel Oppenheimer's poem about the barbers floated through my head the way an aria from *The Barber of Seville* might float through one's consciousness, going in and out, all day long. I heard his poem as I looked out on the fire escape, watching the street life of the ghetto below, searching the figures down there for my missing oldest brother. As I stared down upon the street scene, cars double-parked, people, mostly men, drinking beer and smoking dope, sitting on the stoop of the building, talking about nothing and everything. I thought again of Joel's poem for the barbers. Each word had a resonance, a modal realm (to be jazzy and George Russell-like about it), going through various permutations. The word *tenderly* floated there, or the idea that barbers were *professionals*, and that we should beware (be aware) of them. Thus we grew our hair long, avoiding them entirely, those professionals that they were. We, by contrast, were amateurs, not rank ones, but rather of the serious kind, taking poetry too seriously to make of it a mere profession. *Razor* and *rage* sat there in the mind. I then saw that word *stropping*. This was a word filled with action and intention, almost like an ordinary gesture that might unfold in a drama, only to prove the most noteworthy clue later on. To strop not only had an action associated with it, but it had a context, a scene, an unfolding thereof. We were in a barbershop. Where else did one strop anything? Stropping was rhythmical, slapping a blade, almost like a drummer with a brush to skins, back and forth over the leather strap that was pinned to the side of the barber's chair. You could *smell* the barbery shore this poem hugged. (Don't go into a barbershop if you didn't want a haircut. Or put another way: Daniel did not go back into the lion's den just to get his hat.) You could smell the hair lotion and shaving cream, *see* the combs and brushes, and *hear* the electric whir of the haircutter and, more important, the gossiping and kibitzing clients, doing the Nines with each other. Indeed, if a needle were dug into the head, if a nail were driven into it, could it do any worse damage? (All this was there in Joel's poem about the barbers.) It was the professionals we needed to fear. The professional barbers were simply a metaphor. The professionals we needed to fear ranged from professional poets (at the university), professional journalists (snooping around downtown), professional spies (FBI, CIA, Cointelpro, etc.), professionals in medicine (the dentists and doctors), professional nurses, professional nuns and priests trying to save our souls, professional grandmothers praying for the repose of our souls, professional social workers prowling the streets of the Lower East Side, searching for truants and vagrants (the mythical at-risk youth of the federal grant to St. Mark's Church), drug addled and booze soaked, even professional bartenders (solicitous but insincere), even the professional egg-cream makers throughout this city. Give me the serious amateurs of this community at the corner of Second Avenue and St. Marks Place (and professional proofreaders who would put an apostrophe on St. Marks Place, despite its lacking one on its signage). Give me the serious amateurs at the Poetry Project to the uptown world of professional writing. Give me Ted Berrigan standing in front of Gem Spa, looking into space, thinking, brooding on a new poem. No professional poet wore such an Abrahamic beard. This was a serious amateur, like Joel Oppenheimer was, like all of us were at the Poetry Project. William Carlos Williams was a professional doctor, but the great amateur poet, a kind of lord of amateur poetry, his voice everywhere, influence everywhere and nowhere, his influence there and not there, benign and saturnine, Bacchic and holy, savvy and still filled with wonder, even four years after his death on my birthday in 1963. I sat on my tenement fire escape, staring down East 10th Street at the fray, thinking these and other thoughts, grateful to be where I was, at this time in the world, even a little grateful to be who I was, sitting there on the fire escape, smoking rolled up cigarettes, drinking a can of beer, contemplating the *zeitgeist*, even as my oldest brother was missing in action (MIA), and my friend Diane was nowhere to be found, gone gone, forever and forever. Though no baseball player myself, some of my brothers were very good ones, though none of them were knuckleballers. At Max's Kansas City, Joel Oppenheimer was famous at the bar for two things— his poetry and his slow softball pitch, more a lob than an actual knuckleball, but that no one was able to hit. This is what I was thinking as the sun went down over the Village to the west, the colors dazzling over the Hudson River, filtering through the industrial pollutants of New Jersey, as esthetically pleasing as a Monet painting of the Thames River or the Houses of Parliament. I saw the sun go down over the rooftop of the building on Second Avenue at 10th Street where the poet Sam Abrams and his wife Barbara lived, just as the sun went down on Lewis Warsh and Anne Waldman on St. Marks Place, as it set on Joel and Helen Oppenheimer in the Village, and on everyone else downtown.

III.

WALKING DOWNTOWN

The St. Mark's Poetry Project
is closed for the summer. But
all over the world, poets
are writing poems. Why?

—Ted Berrigan

WALKING DOWNTOWN

1. "I Do This, I Do That"

In the East Village, the beat was still Beat, the rhythm still jazz's, but other things were beginning to be layered over these rhythms and beats. By the start of 1967, a lot of different voices and voicings, different measures and meters (human and cultural), different beats (congas in the park, electric guitars out tenement windows). Breath and syllable, Charles Olson called it. People bopped, slinked and swayed down St. Marks Place, slouching down Second Avenue towards Ratner's deli and the R.O.K. bar and searching for the rough beast of our time. People boogied along, danced, stutter stepped, cakewalked, and rocked through Cooper Square. They kept on trucking, keeping on, they sidled and varmoosed, lindy hopped, bunny bopped, staggered and floated. A younger brother, the one who was an artist and attended the School of Visual Arts on 23rd Street, once told me that I had a swagger in my walk. To swagger is not to saunter, nor is it to be humble. It has a note of arrogance, this word *swagger*. And my bro' was speaking about the present, not the past. In the past, living on 229 East 10th Street, I did not swagger on the streets of the East Village or its bigger sister, the Lower East Side. I was more ninja-like, more clandestine, almost invisible, in fact, I was mostly invisible. People did not walk around me, but through me, or at least it felt that way. Being invisible was my armor against predations on the mean streets, which despite the love children was still at times scary. No, I did not swagger at age twenty; I slid by you. At night I had a different kind of armor, which came out the later the night was, so it was in operation any time I was out past midnight. There I moved through these busy streets like a crazy person, muttering to myself, flailing and twitching. Long ago, growing up in Brooklyn and later out on Long Island, I learnt that the best camouflage was being crazy. Street people thought crazy was contagious, so they stayed away from you. If I was talking to myself, flailing and twitching, almost like the crazy readers at the Monday Night open reading at St. Mark's Church, I had a kind of plenum around me, which was my way of being safe and unaccosted. Swagger came years later, an older person, sober and more vulnerable, maybe coming out of Gleason's gym in Brooklyn, underneath the bridges on Front Street. After two or three hours working out with a trainer, I definitely went outside with swagger, but even then, not so much arrogance as attitude, the self-confidence of knowing how to fight— how to defend myself. Self-defense in the 1960s was more offensive, in the sense of offending, not in the sense of being the aggressor. Everyone I knew was a pacifist. People in the East Village were about the path of least resistance, flowing like water, breathing, transforming, being like the *ronin*, the masterless samurai in the Japan of antiquity. How I walked was determined by all of these qualities, these characteristics, of how to survive, night after night, in a place that was edgy and on edge, peace-loving and dangerous, calm but ready to spring into action. How I walked was an off-shoot or coeval to finding a voice in poetry. How did one strut in a poem?

If I ever came up with a unifying theory about life in downtown Manhattan in the 1960s, it would be the theory of walking, and how it joined up everything—the Poetry Project, Thelonious Monk, the Old Courthouse, the bookstores, bars, workshops, pizzerias and jazz. Walking and poetry, the city and walking; walking to work, walking with friends and writers through the East Village, all of this was not exercise but, as Henry David Thoreau said—rumination. It was even a kind of sauntering, how pilgrims walked when they were on pilgrimages. Frank O'Hara was a past master of walking in the city, and so were an assortment of others in attendance at the Poetry Project, if not in the workshops, then publishing their poems in *The World*. There was not a street south of 14th Street that I had not walked down, hoofing it from my flat on the weekend down to Battery Park and New York Harbor before me, the Staten Island ferry pulling into its landing just as another one took off for that lonely borough in the morning fog hugging the Jersey shoreline. No one could get sentimental and nostalgic for Staten Island, not even Henry David Thoreau, who early in his life spent time there.

By 1968, many of the young writers from the workshops

and also Max's Kansas City would drift over to the St. Adrian Company, a cavernous bar at 763 Broadway near Great Jones Street. Harry Lewis was the jazzy poetry-writing bartender there, and he was liberal with buy-backs for his writer friends. (Meaning: you drank for free all evening.) The fiction writer Joan Silber was a waitress at St. Adrian's. But Joan was not just any waitress; she was a kind of paradigm of the time, someone who knew everyone, was very hip and intelligent, and when not working at the bar obviously doing creative things on her own. As others came and went, Joan was there, almost like Old Faithful, a monument to the place. She was quiet, observant, and thoughtful, taking in everything. She reminded me of that Isaac Babel injunctive: You must know everything. In other words, I had the hunch that nothing escaped her. Joan took everything in from inside and outside of Max's and later from St. Adrian Company bar. She worked there until just about its end a few years later, just before the Broadway Central hotel next door collapsed, taking the bar as a kind of collateral damage. (Thus my bar-tab there seemed to disappear from sight as well, although the owner once asked me, at a book party for Joel Oppenheimer, when I intended to pay my bar tab, and I began speaking to him with a foreign accent, claiming I was not whom he thought I was.) Yet even before one hung out in a place like this artist bar, you sauntered, like other pilgrims, all over the city. The walking was the reason for being, not the bar at the end of the walk, though I certainly over-appreciated the bar, and sometimes I under-appreciated the walking, though not too often did I get negative about the sauntering, the dance of the city, waltzing through its crowds.

My own perambulations through the downtown city often took on a steady arc, a kind of beat, in the sense of a flatfooted cop, but also a musical cadence. From the Old Courthouse at Second Street, I walked up Second Avenue to St. Marks Place and then westward across that thoroughfare, always filled with people, always teeming with the insanity of the moment, weird styles of pastel, tie-dyed dress, the smell of marijuana in the air. Drug-sellers hawked their wares from doorways, runaways shivered on tenement doorsteps, and even the odd celebrity could be seen hanging out—Jimi Hendrix in front of a headshop, Andy Warhol in front of the Electric Circus, Patti Smith or Sam Shepard roaming along that Boulevard of Broken Dreams.

From St. Marks Place I headed further westward through Cooper Square, where the giant metal cube sculpture sat, along with the graffiti inscription on it: Give Me Librium or Give Me Meth. I usually made this trek in late afternoon, then I walked down 8th Street. (I once encountered the young Danny DeVito here, him wearing a cape, looking very *fin de siècle* or vampirish, and he asked me who the hell I was looking at. "Not you, you little twerp," I said, and he burst out laughing wildly, saying, "You're all right.") Between Lafayette Street and

Broadway, there was a canyon effect from the buildings, and the wind invariably howled and whistled for that one long block until I got onto Eighth Street proper, and the wind diminished. From there it was only two long blocks until I arrived at the Eighth Street Bookshop to work the night shift from six in the evening until midnight.

After work in the bookshop, people went to the Lion's Head to hang out with Joel Oppenheimer, if someone had money to burn. Otherwise, it was back to the East Village, reversing the songline, walking back along Eighth Street to St. Marks Place, then down Second Avenue to the Old Courthouse or, later, to Ron Edson's new apartment on East 1st Street. In the way that New York School poets hung out at Anne and Lewis' apartment on St. Marks Place, the poets from Joel's workshop seemed to hang out at Ron and Nicki's place. Somehow Ron would get up in the morning, and then go teach in a junior high school in Midtown. How he did this, I will never know.

The next morning, I would go out and walk again, being universally broke, like everyone else, so the only other form of entertainment I had was the cheap revival movie houses that showed a double-bill of art-house films, mostly European, though sometimes Japanese, for only a few dollars. I went to museums when I could and if they were free, invariably walking everywhere, and my orbit included, as it did for most other downtown poets, the world between the two rivers, but always that lower part of Manhattan Island. I might drift down to Battery Park and take a Staten Island ferry, reading Walt Whitman aloud to myself or even recite Ginsberg's "Howl" for the perplexed commuters.

Clearly the urge for walking and poetry, for walking and thoughts on one's city, was not new to the poets at the Poetry Project and other writers in downtown Manhattan in the late Sixties. The nature of New York made it a walker's city, unlike Los Angeles where walking is literally a crime in some neighborhoods. (In 1968, housesitting for a friend in Venice, California, I was arrested by the police after I went out to buy some wine and beer. My crime? I was walking, and I used to have, for show, the ticket they gave me, on which it was written: Walking.) Downtown Manhattan especially lent itself to this enterprise, this rumination that writers underwent, sauntering as if on pilgrimage. The Objectivist poet Charles Reznikoff was legendary for his long walks from the Bronx deep into Manhattan, and even over to Brooklyn and back home again, even when he was well into old age. Reznikoff's poetic was not just a language of place, but of perambulation, a kind of snapshot Imagism that took in things on the hoof, at the accelerated pace of the impassioned walker.

Reznikoff has a poem, in which he enters a laundry to pick up a shirt, only to discover that it is missing. The owner tells him that there are four ways to look at it. It may never have been delivered. It might be lying there, unpacked. It may have been put into someone else's bundle. Or it may really be lost. The laundryman tells the poet to come back in a week. The wife of the laundryman comes forward: "We won't have to go to the rabbi about it, will we?" It seems to me that only a poet who walked a lot could have written that poem. The sedentary writer would never have been in such a location or, if she or he were, they might not even notice the poetic nature of the moment, the poem as it were unfolding before them. There is a rhythm to walking, therefore, and there is a rhythm to a walking poem. There is a rhythm to walking prose, too. I think of James Joyce's *Ulysses* as a great perambulating novel, the walker in the city, moving about in the world. It is by drunkenly walking into each other that Stephen Daedalus and Leopold Bloom meet up in Dublin.

Yet one does not make poetry merely by walking, just as the French poet Mallarmé said to the painter Degas, one did not make poetry with ideas, but with *words*. Even with walking, words were needed, and a certain relationship to them, beyond mere didactic meanings into the realm of pure sound. So perhaps walking in downtown New York brought forth a sense of pure sound, a cacophony that merged into music, just the way the discordant notes of the city were harnessed and shaped into the piano notes by Thelonious Monk. Certainly one cannot think of a Poetry Project at St. Mark's Church without considering Thelonious Monk at the Five Spot.

The most iconic poem that young poets read at the Poetry Project was Frank O'Hara's poem "The Day Lady

Died," about Billie Holiday's death. The St. Mark's poets would do an endless theme and variation on this poem, for instance, so many of Ted Berrigan's own poetry references O'Hara's poem; either directly, by quoting its lines, or assuming its perambulating rhythms. Frank O'Hara was the quintessential walking poet of New York City, the paradigm for everyone else, especially in his book *Lunch Poems* (1964). His walking obsession is chronicled in poem after poem in that book. In one of those poems, he refers to a book of poems by Pierre Reverdy, which was in his pocket. For me, walking around downtown New York, it was not so much Pierre Reverdy as it was O'Hara's *Lunch Poems*, which seemed to be with me everywhere I walked.

But how do we know Frank O'Hara is walking in those poems? Well, for instance, he tells us so in the second stanza of the Billie Holiday poem: "I walk up the muggy street beginning to sun," and he eats a hamburger and drinks a malted and buys a literary magazine. But O'Hara is uptown at work, not downtown with the jazz, the painters, the poets, *the action*. He walks to the bank, to a bookshop called the Golden Griffin, and buys a book for a friend. After buying Strega in a liquor store, he walks back to Sixth Avenue, and goes to the tobacconist in the Ziegfeld Theatre for two cartons of European cigarettes. "The Day Lady Died" is a poem, it seems, about life and death, but it arrives at its destination by the act of walking. Walking in Midtown Manhattan, Frank O'Hara sees the

New York Post headline about the singer Billie Holiday's death. Walking had taken him uptown to work, but invariably it led him, by way of his thoughts and feelings, back downtown among his friends, and into places like the Five Spot Café.

But in my walking in those days back in the sixties, I was not thinking about Frank O'Hara but Ezra Pound. When I ran away from home, age fifteen, I one day purchased a used hardcover copy of Ezra Pound's book, *The Cantos*, one of the few possessions I still had. My interest in Ezra Pound began with the purchase of that epic poem from a Lower East Side bookshop. I knew he was controversial during World War II, broadcasting what later were deemed "treasonable" speeches from Italy, which landed him in jail in Italy after the war and then later put him on trial in America and, eventually, got him incarcerated in St. Elizabeths Hospital for the criminally insane in Washington, D.C. Pound was more insane than criminal, but that distinction seemed irrelevant to where he wound up. Something Pound said kept dogging me in those days on the Lower East Side, particularly as I was out walking, the endless walking I did, not exercising, but ruminating, like Thoreau said in his essay "Walking." This is what I kept ruminating about. Pound wrote: "Poetry should be written at least as well as prose." I don't know why this stuck in my head but it did. Suddenly there was a lot more talk of Ezra Pound at the Poetry Project because I was attending workshops given by Sam Abrams, as Joel's classes had become erratic. Sam knew a lot about *The Cantos* and though he was Jewish, he would engage me with conversations about Pound.

"Sam," I said.

"Yeah, Machine Gun," he answered, since that is what Joel and he called me.

"If poetry had to be at least as well written as prose," I said, "doesn't that mean that prose was better written than poetry?"

2.   Thelonious Sphere Monk

O ften, when the weather was nice or even sometimes when it wasn't nice at all, I would walk after work. New York City is more like Hong Kong than London or Paris or Rome because it is a city of various islands. Both Brooklyn and Queens are on Long Island; Staten Island is on, well, Staten Island. Only the Bronx is situated on the mainland of the United States, the rest of it, almost like Greece, a ribbon, a necklace of archipelagoes or islands are different than mainland, and island people are different than mainlanders too. Think of Japan or the United Kingdom; think of Ireland. All of these islands and their islanders are different than the people in the hills, the people in the mountains, those in dusty towns on the Plains in the middle of America. I have walked from the southern tip of Manhattan by the ferry docks all the way up to Spuyten Duyvil. It is a thirteen mile journey, but it is not easy to go from south of the city to its north without making side trips east and west. I liked clearing my head after work at the music library, walking down Broadway until I arrived at Union Square and therefore Max's Kansas City, just north of that urban square just below Park Avenue South. But my favorite walks were always below 14th Street, that Maginot line that separated the hip from the square, the queer from the straight, the stoned from the sober, the creative from the mundane. There were no writing workshops or readings, nothing at the Poetry

Project that evening. I did not feel like reading or writing or lying around the apartment, so I walked west on 10th Street, crossed Second Avenue, then walked on that short diagonal street that cut between 9th and 10th streets, and found myself on the Bowery. A very short block south, and I came to the corner of St. Marks Place, crossed this busy interchange, and stepped inside the tiny, cozy, dark, smoked-filled space of the Five Spot Café. The whole process took me less than five minutes to walk to. I ordered a beer and waited for Thelonious Monk to show. I was in the mood for his music that night. When he did show up—of course, many hours late, which I knew he would, which is why I went there so late myself—he came up to the bar to get a drink and saw me and said hello.

"Where you get that lid?" he asked me, referring to my cap.

"Place on Fourth Street," I said, referring to a little shop near Broadway, where I often bought my hats.

"I got to get me one of them," he said. "Why you wear so many hats? You copying me, Kid?"

"My grandfather was a hatmaker," I told him. "He was a haberdasher."

"Nah," Monk said.

"Yeah," I said. "His factory was just down the road, at Broadway and Houston. There's still a big sign on the side of the building."

"What's his name?"

"Drew," I said.

But then someone distracted him, one of his sidemen that night, asking him a question about the order of the music, and Monk walked away. Until that moment, it had been the longest we had ever engaged one another in conversation. I ordered another beer, I lit myself a cigarette, I put on my sunglasses, I pulled down the brim of my hat, I hunched up the collar on my jacket, I scrunched down on my barstool, I opened my ears to get ready to listen to Thelonious Sphere Monk. He walked up to the piano, sat down, and began to play immediately, a ballad, one I did not know, and after a while, his quartet joined the master, and they began to play "Nutty," followed by "Monk's Dream" and "Round Midnight." It was that kind of evening, Monk very lively and astutely musical, the room filled up with people who knew his music quite well. I often wondered how I became friendly with Monk, and why he chose to talk to me, of all the people present at the Five Spot Café. I was not a musician. He was at least thirty years my senior. He was a Black man; I was a white kid, though I did identify more with Black culture (musically, visually, fashionwise, and in terms of poetry, LeRoi Jones' angry, streetwise poems my anthems, the poetry that touched me most deeply). Other than my visceral response to his music, I had no credentials to evaluate Monk. I simply loved what I heard, found it corresponded to a rhythmical noise in my own human universe, i.e., the shaped and random, the quick and slow, the randomness of my own mind and its rhythms. For my part, I understood why I liked Monk personally. He was certainly the coolest person I'd ever met. I liked his observations, his sly humor, his humanity, and his intelligence. I had left home around the same age he did. We were the same height. We were both former basketball players. (Years later, reading Robin Kelley's biography of Monk, I would learn that Monk was also deemed schizophrenic, something that ran in my own family, two of my brothers living with that diagnosis.) We were New Yorkers. Outsiders. My own goofy sense of humor was mirrored in that music. I had a goatee and wore hats. Monk could see that I was very animated about my passion for his sound. Put into the parlance of the time, I had a lot to identify with there. Monk's music was as big an influence upon my writing as Frank O'Hara or Joel Oppenheimer's poetry. When I walked around the city, roaming aimlessly or purposefully heading to some venue to meet friends, usually Thelonious Monk's music flowed through my head and was even in my muscles and sinews.

The Five Spot Cafe, where Thelonious Monk played eternally onward into the night, was about to be transformed from a legendary jazz club into a pizza parlor. The Termini brothers, its owners, had had enough of the jazzy nightlife and wanted a respite. In the run up to their closing, I would go there to hear Thelonious Monk: he was now too big for such a tiny club, but he still came down to hang out, which meant sitting in with whomever was playing, whether it was Roswell Rudd or Charles Mingus. The new Five Spot Cafe only lasted three years on St. Marks Place, mainly because the main thoroughfare through the East Village had become a stoners' paradise, a long alleyway of perdition and rock 'n' roll. Jazz was something that old people, academics, and poets listened to, not the new generation, the hippies and drugged out drifters even replacing the more traditional—I almost want to say classical—tramps, winos, and hoboes, who once frequented this part of Third Avenue known as the Bowery, New York's Skid Row until a few minutes earlier when it had transformed itself into a happening place, like just about everything else below 14th Street.

Thelonious Monk once told his sax player, Charlie Rouse, not to pay attention to what Monk himself was playing in rehearsal because once they were in front of an audience or in the studio recording sides, Monk was going to play something completely different. I find this observation to be no truer than on a Columbia recording of "Monk's Dream," and all one need to do is to listen carefully to Charlie Rouse playing the tune, and then listen beyond the tune to Monk doing backup ("comping"). What he is playing has literally nothing to do with Rouse's music. I should say that it seems to have nothing to do with what Charlie Rouse's saxophone is doing—playing the tune—until the piece progresses, and finally Monk joins his mishegoss to the actual mood of the piece, proving once again that the rhythm was so deeply ingrained in his soul and consciousness, that he didn't need to play melody per se, but rather could play around it, play everything but the tune and the melody and the rhythm, though eventually he would wind up in the same place as Charlie Rouse, Frankie Dunlop, and John Ore, because the melody had been there all along, if only suspended in his mind until he was ready to snatch it back to life again.

Ornette Coleman, quoted in A.B. Spellman's *Four Lives in the Bebop Business*, said that Monk was "the master of taking the chord change of a tune and playing a different melodic line on top of it." Besides Monk's technical virtuosity and allusive stride on the piano, Cecil Taylor said that Monk could "jar you emotionally." Downtown, in the late 1960s, everyone seemed to be reading A. B. Spellman's book. He had been one of the managers at the Eighth Street Bookshop, and besides his wise take on jazz in his prose, he was a gifted poet. All of the jazz innovators whom Spellman interviewed and wrote about spoke about Monk as a key influence. Charlie Parker had called Monk "deep," while Art Blakey went one step further and said that Monk was "the guy who started it all." The British poet Philip Larkin referred to Monk as a personality "who disdained the daylight of success," but he also noted "Monk's thrashing feet and gnomic comments, together with his tendency to do a shuffle-dance, hands outstretched from the keyboard, all round the Five Spot (ending at the bar), constitute a kind of moonlight exhibitionism." Larkin, otherwise wise and gifted as a critic and poet, seemed to have a tin-ear for Thelonious Monk, even going so far as to call his piano-playing "ham-fisted." Suffice it to say, the British never did understand Thelonious Monk. Except for a few enlightened musicians, they did not *get* Monk.

I dwell on Thelonious Monk because his music had an influence upon the young writers whom I knew, myself included. Myself particularly. I was damn-near obsessed with Monk's music, going to hear him every chance I had, and whenever I had some extra cash, I went over to the Five Spot a few blocks away or, if he were playing in the Village, I walked across 8th Street until I went across Washington Square Park to the Village Gate on Bleecker Street or, more often, the Village Vanguard on Seventh Avenue South. As popular as Monk had become in the 1960s, he was still a misunderstood composer and pianist, even among his peers, and the odd-man-out piano player in various groups from the bebop era. During the 1950s, Monk developed his enormous talent in isolation. Fame did not come to him the way it came to other jazzmen from the previous decade and earlier. The lack of recognition made him more eccentric perhaps—the hats, the shades, the booze, the drugs—but it also allowed him to refine the musical experiments he started years earlier. When the sixties rolled around, Monk was getting attention, and had even become a celebrity in downtown

New York City, if not across the country and in the world the way Louis Armstrong or Dizzy Gillepsie were. He left Riverside records to become one of the stars at Columbia; not only was he one of that record label's main attractions, he became, in 1964, a pop culture phenomenon when his hip, enigmatic countenance graced perhaps the most astounding cover of *Time* magazine. I also dwell on Thelonious Monk because I loved his music. His is the music, as I have already noted, that rang out in my head as I walked from my flat on East 10th Street to work or, later in the evening, to a poetry reading or a writing workshop. Improvisation was the spirit of the 1960s, and Monk was its paradigm. Yet I realize that Monk's music was not in everyone's heads. More than likely, and more often than not, the new rock music was in their heads. Jimi Hendrix, for instance, or Janice Joplin, Eric Clapton, the Rolling Stones, the Doors, even the Beatles. James Brown might have been in their heads or some Motown group, Smokey Robinson, perhaps, or Marvin Gaye, the latter becoming really fine as the Sixties progressed. But I dwell on Thelonious for more than personal and improvisational reasons. In many respects, the 1960s was Monk's era, even though he honed his pianistic virtues in the 1930s on the road and during the 1940s in Harlem. I was fortunate to have heard Monk so early in my life. I would play an album in my railroad flat on East 10th Street in the morning before going off to work uptown, or I alternated a Monk album with listening to WBAI radio for the news and weather, and would listen to my Monk albums again when I came home at night, when I played another album. Wherever I walked downtown, whether in the East Village, the Village, the Lower East Side, Chinatown, or Little Italy, I heard Monk's music in my head, and my walk, my stride, my perambulatory shuffle, was all determined and influenced by Thelonious Sphere Monk. Thus Monk's music was always there in the air, a part of the East Village's conversation, a part of its chemistry. Sometimes, too, meeting one of my older brothers, who worked as a stagehand at the Metropolitan Opera House next to the music library, we adjourned to the Century Bar on Amsterdam Avenue, and if Monk was in town, I saw him outside the bar, talking to his lifelong friends and neighbors, as he had literally grown up on those intense streets behind the newly opened Lincoln Center.

I also saw him late at night on St. Marks Place in front of the Five Spot Café, either smoking a cigarette outside or sitting in the Rolls Royce Silver Cloud owned by the Countess Rothchild, who was his patron. As always, as ever, Thelonious Monk wore an elegant, shimmering suit and tie, a silk scarf around his neck against the chill, and a felt hat on his head. His overcoat was cashmere. He wore alligator loafers and sheer socks, as he shuffled off. If you knew his music as I did, you knew that he walked in the exact rhythm of his music, hesitatingly lyrical, bouncing and cacophonous, full of the new and future, though alluding to the past (the old piano players from Harlem and the Deep South, Kansas City and Chicago), a human encyclopedia of jazz ideas and innovations. I thought of gun fighters walking off into the sunset in the old West, only this was the Upper West Side, San Juan Hill, the new West with Lincoln Center across the road, and instead of being a gunslinger, Monk was the innovative piano player and composer, one of the inventors, therefore, of the 1960s, at least for me. Thelonious Monk was still my idea of a paradigm for the improvisational, the spontaneous, the new, the experimental, purely American, Black, African American, all the things young writers aspired to in their poems, what all of us were downtown to do, to be like he be, have that certain kind of strut, not so much a swagger, a bounce, like the basketball players in the playground at Sixth Avenue and West 3rd Street in the Village, like LeRoi Jones in his poetry or Ornette Coleman on his plastic saxophone. We wanted to be like Thelonious Monk, if not the sharkskin suits and the pointy loafers with the transparent black socks, then with the cool hats he wore, his goatee, but mainly, his being who he was, the man he be, the one he was, Thelonious Sphere Monk.

Now I saw Monk downtown, in front of the Five Spot Cafe, not performing—he was too big to play there now—but just hanging out with old friends, including the Termini brothers who owned the place. The Baronness' limo was parked outside on St. Marks Place, a few tramps and hippies eyeing it either with suspicion or awe. Uptown, I would run into Monk on the backside of Lincoln Center, in San Juan Hill, his 'hood. Standing in front of the Century bar seemed to be his preferred spot, so if I was meeting my brother there, I said hello to Monk before I went inside. Sometimes he said hello; but more usually he simply looked at me, wondering who I was. Once I even said, "We spoke a few times at the Five Spot." "Oh, yeah," he said, but there was a blank look in his face, as if he didn't remember it at all. "You used to call me the Kid," I said, but that made no impression on him at all, so I said goodbye and walked into the Century to look for my brother Peter, the stagehand at the Metropolitan Opera House. When he took a break, he often went into the Century for a beer.

About the time that Diane left for good, my oldest brother Jimmy showed up full of mania, genius, energy, and madness, i.e., he fit in beautifully in the East Village. At the flat he drank a case of beer each day, consumed a half gallon of bourbon, and smoked about eighty Pall Mall cigarettes each day. He was always a big man, even when he was a boy. Barrel-chested, strong, and a great fighter, he'd been thrown out of the Army for one of his manic escapades in Spain. When he was in the midst of his own mania, there was a genius to everything my brother did, so that his conversations were like works of art. He would go from the war in Vietnam to potatoes displayed at the green grocer's on First Avenue, the poetry of Joel Oppenheimer to Hemingway's writing set in Spain. (When he got in trouble in Europe, he had been AWOL from a base in Germany, having the time of his life pretending to be Ernest Hemingway in *The Sun Also Rises*, and my brother did resemble Papa Hemingway, albeit forty-three years younger than his literary hero.) At my flat, he drank beer around the clock, calling it "holy water," and ate pizzas and Chinese take-out, sausage sandwiches and corn beef on Jewish rye with mustard dripping off the sides, he inveighed against the establishment and vowed to live out his days the way Maxwell Bodenheim had lived, writing poems, drinking cheap wine, and getting stabbed in a Bowery hotel over someone stealing his wine bottle. (We had such ambitions in my family, our Irish Romany blood obvious in these so-called goals.)

The brother, as brothers do, had received about twenty-five shock treatments at Valley Forge Hospital in Pennsylvania. He was given a dishonorable discharge, and came back to Long Island a broken man. He was in his mid-twenties. Lethargy was his middle name; he seemed to be swimming in a sea of molasses. In many respects, his mania was a welcome event, taking him from the darkest corners of hell in the bright lights, not of Broadway, but his very mania. For the longest time he sat in a reclining chair in the family's living room, smoking cigarettes and staring into space. Then he began to walk around and go down to the caddy shack at the local golf course to play poker. He walked to the golf course and back, about two or three miles each way. Eventually he moved to Connecticut, to hang with a childhood friend, but wound up living with a bunch of former professional (really semi-professional) football players. They had a high tolerance for my brother, but even they tired of him, and that's how he appeared at my door, a case of beer under his arm, a couple of sausage and sweet onion sandwiches in a bag, a kind of spiritual offering to coincide with his arrival.

We immediately stopped by the Five Spot Café. Maybe Monk might show up, and he did one night, and my brother and Monk confabbed, but I couldn't hear what they said to each other. I think they were comparing notes about being locked up on flight decks in various hospitals. This is how I imagined they responded to each other: "That Monk," my brother said. "That brother of yours," Monk said. "That motherfucker's been around." My brother had been traveling through various parallel universes ever since I met him in Brooklyn. Of my parents sixteen children, I am the only one not born in St. Mary's Hospital in Weeksville, Bedford-Stuyvesant; I was born in Washington, D.C., just after the Second World War ended. The whole time I lived in Greenbelt, Maryland, my two oldest brothers, Jimmy and Peter, were growing up in Flatbush at my uncle's half-a-house at Flatlands and Avenue L. My two older brothers welcomed me to Marion Street by placing a pillow over my face, either pretending to execute me via not being able to breathe or just pretending to intimidate me into subjection to their collective wills. In either case, I was terrified of them.

One night Jimmy and I went over to the Five Spot, and Charles Mingus was performing. Years later, I wrote this poem:

MINGUS AT THE FIVE SPOT

I heard Mingus at the Five Spot Café
After it moved from the Bowery to
The corner at St. Marks Place, hot summer
Night, I was with my oldest brother James,
He then called himself, though I had known him
All my life as Jimmy. He was going
Through a brilliant manic phase of his life,
And stayed as a guest at my East 10th Street
Apartment just around the corner, and
Mingus, in a surly mood, removed cats
From his band who weren't carrying their
Loads, then he asked audience members to
Leave, but he overlooked my big, loud bro',
Claiming we all were more appreciative.

Now Jimmy was in my tiny apartment, pronouncing from the fire escape, shouting poems, scribbling in my various poetry books his manic observations. My old copy of Joel Oppenheimer's *Love Bit* was scribbled over with my brother's notes: *Is Joel Oppenheimer the Johnny*

Unitas of poets? Training along. Training too long. In the background, the Raylettes saying, "Yes, it is, yes, it is." The second longest day of the year. Within the week, I left my brother at the corner of First Avenue and East 10th Street, as he jumped on the back of a garbage truck going uptown, Jimmy holding on with one hand as he waved crazily with the other. I would learn, many months later from him, that the garbage men, seeing him on the back of the truck, drove right to Bellevue hospital, where they deposited my brother onto the flight deck, and he remained until he was given a diagnosis of paranoid schizophrenia, with manic depression. Years later, talking about this episode, my brother said: "If you are a big guy and you wind up in Bellevue, they always give you that diagnosis. It doesn't mean anything. It's just another label."

I remembered something my oldest brother had said to me before he jumped on the back of the garbage truck. He had drunk so much that he had drunk himself sober. He sat by the window overlooking 10th Street, smoking a cigarette, and then asked me: "What do you want to do with your poetry, Michael?" I didn't know how to answer him. Then it came to me: Monk was what I wanted my poetry to sound like. He had found the rhythm of the city in his music. Now I had to figure out a way to put such rhythms into my poetry and prose.

3.   The Eighth Street Bookshop

Being out of work now, I fell behind in my rent by a month or two, and my Ukrainian landlord was not pleased. He threatened to throw my possessions out on the street if I didn't give him at least a partial payment of the rent. I told him that he couldn't do that; it was illegal. "You watch and see," he said, "if I can't do it. If I don't have my rent, you'll be out on your ass." The landlord, who was Ukrainian, sounded exactly like Benya Krik, Isaac Babel's Jewish gangster anti-hero from Odessa. "If I don't have my money, Eichbaum, you won't have your cows." But instead of Eichbaum and his cows, it was M. G. Stephens and the rent arrears. I came back to the apartment after walking all over the Village and East Village looking for a new job. I saw a bunch of people milling around the stoop to my building.

All my things—my clothes, my books, my pots and pans—were out on the street. There were a few albums still there, the others, including all my Thelonious Monk records, all my jazz albums, were gone, having been scavenged earlier in the day by my neighbors and others passing down East 10th Street. I stood there holding an album cover of Odetta, the record no longer there. My Thelonious Monk records, which I had taken five years to accumulate, going back to when I was fifteen years old, a runaway who had just heard Monk performing at a venue—not the Five Spot—on St. Marks Place, my pilfered Monk albums left a giant record-player shaped hole in my existence. There were maybe twenty-five Monk albums that had been scavenged and looted. I walked away since there was no point going upstairs if everything I owned was out on the street. For the next ten years I would live here and there on every street from 1st to 14th, sleeping on couches, on floors, in chairs, sometimes even for extended periods, upwards of a year. I kept thinking about my Monk albums, dispersed, possessed by others, theirs, no longer mine.

It was in 1967 that I became homeless, moving from place to place, including abandoned buildings, a family tradition because one of my younger brothers, Joe, was an art student at the School of Visual Arts, and he squatted, along with some of his fellow students, an empty building on Canal Street, right across from the tunnel to New Jersey. I spent a few nights there, more than a few nights at my poetry friend Ron Edson's various apartments on Sullivan Street in the Village and then East 1st Street, where I often went to take a shower and get some breakfast or just to hang out with Ron, Sonny (a runaway from Brooklyn whom Tom Weatherly seemed to adopt), Tom himself, and others from the Poetry Project. I first got into a reading jag on Henry David Thoreau while staying at Ron and Nicki's 1st Street apartment. I would look at myself in a tiny mirror over the sink in the bathroom and say aloud: "I, M. G. Stephens, do not wish to be regarded as a member of any incorporated society which

I have not joined." Edson called out: "Are you all right in there, Stephens?" I shouted affirmatively. Then I quoted Thoreau: "I quietly declare war with the state, after my fashion, though I will still make what use and get what advantage of her I can, as is usual in such cases." Besides this political stance—I described myself as a Catholic anarchist, just as I might rightly do so still today—the book reading and the poetry writing, the jazz records and my general attitude, my stance, my very being, if you will, was glued together by a fuzzy thing called hipness—of being cool. But the Catholic anarchy was concrete, not a vague believe. Right next to Ron and Nicki's apartment was Dorothy Day's Catholic Worker storefront, and I would regularly see Dorothy there. Like with my nodding friendship with Thelonious Monk, I regularly said hello to Dorothy, though I did occasionally, especially when drunk, engage her in conversation, even submitting some of my poetry to the *Catholic Worker* newspaper, which she edited. "Your poems remind me of Gene's early poems," she once told me. I asked, "Who the fuck is Gene?" She looked at and through me, as if I were an incorporeal angel or spirit. There are many who believe that Dorothy was a saint, a real Catholic saint, and so I can boast that I often hugged and kissed on the cheek a human being who was also an American Catholic potential saint. Of course, I would learn, Gene was her old boyfriend, the playwright Eugene O'Neill. It was Dorothy who advised me about war resisting, and she introduced me to someone who also

131

advised me about how to deal with further draft notices, dragging me down to Whitehall Street for physicals or as this friend of Dorothy Day advised me, "you are just fodder for the war machine to the people at Whitehall."

The counter-measure to the Monk shuffle or the spontaneously rendered poem of performance came in the heavy measures of the Draft Board, which once again wanted me to come in for a physical. My second draft notice told me to report to Whitehall Street, which I had to do, I figured, because they had my forwarding address to Ron's place on 1st, where they could find me if I decided not to show. Whitehall was located downtown near the Battery, in the financial district of the city, a world away from what I am describing about the downtown world of the Village, East Village, and the Lower East Side. Whitehall was the military, where young men were conscripted and inducted, transformed overnight into killing machines. Whitehall was young men lined up in hallways in their underpants, holding paperwork to take to the next station of their physical; it was cold feet on the marble floors, a chill in the air. Whitehall was older men with dead eyes looking at us young men like we were not so much human as hunks of meat or just plain fodder, like that Catholic Worker person said to me, for the war machine. I did not like Whitehall at all.

During this period, I read and reread Thoreau's essay, "On the Duty of Civil Disobedience." How I approached my draft notice had a lot to do with my reading of this essay. In it, Thoreau writes that "if injustice is part of the necessary friction of the machine of government, let it go, let it go; perchance it will wear smooth—certainly the machine will wear out." He goes on to observe:

If the injustice has a spring, or a pulley, or a rope, or a crank, exclusively for itself then perhaps you may consider whether the remedy will not be worse than the evil; but if it is of such a nature that it requires you to be the agent of injustice to another, then, I say, break the law. Let your life be a counter friction to stop the machine. What I have to do is to see, at any rate, that I do not lend myself to the wrong which I condemn.

Muhammad Ali had put it best when he resisted being drafted himself. The heavyweight boxing champion of the world had given his reason for not wanting to fight in the American military as follows: "Man, I ain't got no quarrel with the Vietcong." Of all the African American leaders of the 1960s, Ali was the most dynamic figure. Almost like yin and yang, I put him in a pantheon with Martin Luther King. Of course, Ali was yin and yang combined, politically a pacifist, but professionally a pugilist. Many people found this hypocritical; I found it inspirational. He was the living testament of what someone at an anti-war rally in Syracuse tried to show me, that being a pacifist politically was not contradictory to a warrior mentality elsewhere, for instance, in the boxing ring, a sport with rules and regulations passed down through the 19th century by the Marquis of Queensbury. Between Ali and King, both of whom I greatly admired for different reasons, I would have to put Malcom X, the newly fallen (assassinated in Harlem) Muslim leader who had defected from Elijah Mohammad's strain of the religion to become more traditionally Islamic after going on the Hajj in Mecca. I was never enamored by the cult of the Kennedys, so even though I was Irish, I didn't see them in my political altar of saints and celebrities. Along with King and Ali and X, I had Dorothy Day, who I thought was a white-haired living saint, roaming the streets of the East Village, helping young people like myself to resist the escalating war. With this pantheon in my head, I thought of Thoreau's "Civil Disobedience" again.

"Any man more right than his neighbors," he wrote, "constitutes a majority of one already."

At Whitehall, standing in the freezing corridor in my underwear and socks, holding the paperwork for the next station of my physical, I was a majority of one, I thought, and like Thoreau, my quarrel was with men and not with parchment. He also wrote things that appealed to the black and white nature of my twenty-something mind. I was not yet experienced enough in the world to know that most of life is lived in gray areas, neither right nor wrong, good nor bad. Therefore I loved Thoreau for writing: "Absolutely speaking, the more money, the less virtue." This seemed especially true in the extreme downtown economic parishes where the financiers and capitalists plied their trade. Compared to their extravagant life styles, I lived a monkish existence in the East Village, practicing the craft of writing at night and in the earliest hours of the morning. I would drink my morning tea, eating a piece of toast, preparing myself to go to out and find a new job. I did not have to shave or wash my hair, my beard and hair being birds' nests of tangles and curls, so I could think about Thoreau writing that he could afford to refuse allegiance to Massachusetts. I could afford to refuse allegiance to America, I thought, because its war is unjust, its policies are corrupt, its politicians are spineless orators defending corporations over people.

That is how I walked down to Whitehall Street and into my physical for the military draft, full of an agitation created from reading Thoreau's pamphlet. I was prepared to deliver an excoriating speech to the people at the Draft Board. But I never really got to say anything. Once again my bloodwork was awful, mainly from smoking the opiated hash, and my heartbeat was irregular. But instead of giving me a 4-F, I was once again rated 1-Y, not yet fit for purpose, militarily speaking. I walked back to the East Village triumphant, feeling like a Roman conqueror. Words were powerful, I thought. Thoreau had filled me full of purpose. I was a non-violent pacifist to my core; I was anti-war, anti-establishment, anti-government, anti-family, anti-literature, anti-poetry. I liked going to a tiny boxing gym around 13th Street, to work out and spar. I was nothing if not full of contradictions. It reminded me of a Henry Miller quip when he lived in Paris, about having no money and no hope and being the happiest man alive. As I walked north from Whitehall, I was the happiest person alive. Eventually I crossed Houston Street near Second Avenue, back into my area of operation, my warren. I imagined walking past the Old Courthouse, which was locked up and silent at this time of day except for maybe a theater group rehearsing a play. I walked past the Italian cemetery and funeral parlor, past the movie theaters, Ratner's, the ROK bar, crossed St. Marks Place and turned right onto East 10th Street and up the four flights of stairs in my tenement, unlocking my door and stepping inside. But it was only a dream; I had been smoking too much opiated hash. I no longer lived at 229 East 10th Street, having unceremoniously been evicted for rent arrears. During my time on East 10th, I had several roommates who helped to pay the rent. The first was my childhood friend Jamie, who would go on to become a light technician expert at the Public Theater on Lafayette Street. Another was Jules from Joel's workshop, but more political provocateur than poet. I had smoked so much hash that I saw him in the apartment too.

"How did it go, M.G.?"

"Well, I didn't flunk the physical, Jules," I said. "But I didn't pass with flying honors either. They made me 1-Y again."

"Mazel tov," he said. "We'll show the pigs."

I sat down on my mattress on the floor of the front

room, took out my stick of hash, cut off a piece and placed it in my pipe, lit it up and inhaled deeply. The seam between dream and reality disintegrated. I put on one of my Thelonious Monk records, "Straight, No Chaser," and lay back on the pillow, listening to his piano fill the room. But when I came to later that day in which I had received another deferment on my draft status, Jules and Jamie and 10th Street were gone, and in reality I was sat on a couch in Ron and Nicki's living room.

"Are you all right?" Ron asked.

"I need to stop smoking this shit," I said. "Maybe I should go for a walk."

Of course, my job at the music library ended because my pipe smoking had fucked with my sense of time. In fact, time did not exist, just some other kind of dimension in space, and even that was questionable. Spatially I was on another planet. That is when I stopped going to my job at Lincoln Center after a year, which is how I got evicted. I still attended the poetry workshops at the church in the Old Courthouse around the corner from Ron and Nicki's apartment. Besides the thousands of *Alcohol Poems* I was writing, I started to write some prose, just a little here and there, mostly about working in the Merchant Marines a year and a half earlier.

I now had a job working off the books for a tiny bookshop on Avenue B called the Tompkins Square Bookshop. They also had a literary magazine called the Tompkins Square Review, which featured a lot of the

Beat writers like Ray Bremser and a younger generation of heroin poets like Clive Matson. The writer Michael Perkins was the editor of the magazine. I ran the bookshop in the daylight hours for the Pooles, a married couple who owned the bookshop.

I began to travel very lightly, with only a book or two, with my poetry manuscripts in a spring binder; it was a sign that I was the real deal. I had become a vagabond poet, in the tradition of the Zen poets, drinking and spouting poetry, with no fixed abode. It was not so much the kindness of strangers that saved me, as the mutually stoned conditions all of us were in, making such an invitation for me to stay the night an unconscious act, though to be sure, there was often love and kindness behind these gestures. Eventually I lived in the abandoned courthouse building at Second Avenue and 2nd Street where the Poetry Project held its workshops. In fact, it was those workshops that became the only anchor in my otherwise rudderless life. I wrote, I walked everywhere, I smoked, I brooded, I shouted, I drank, I starved, I argued into the night, shouting at the stars and the moon. Imagine Monk's "Nutty" or "Epistrophy" as the themes to this story.

When I walked past the Five Spot Café on St. Marks Place, it was now a pizza parlor, the slices actually pretty good. But that great music which cascaded out of there was no more. A giant pizza oven stood where the bar once was—Thelonious Monk drinking a shot of whiskey and smoking a cigarette, talking to me about basketball and the weather—this was now a memory in my mind. The saddest thing of all was how the hippies came in and ordered pizza slices, without a thought to what this place used to be, a Mecca, the Holy See, Albion, the place of jazz. Now that I was officially homeless, I sauntered in a manner like the winos and bums on the Bowery. Mostly I slept on friends' couches and floors. Occasionally I sat all night in a coffeehouse, reading a book, writing in a journal, waiting for the new day and the chance to find someone to let me take a shower. That is how I came to sleep on every street, from 1st to 14th, and from the Bowery over to the East River. But after a few nights, usually I had to move on. When I left a place, I began one of my endless walks from morning to night, most often east to west, going from the poverty and rootlessness of the East Village to the more affluent and stable warrens in the Village.

Thank God for the Poetry Project, I thought, because even as I became bereft of poetry, my compeers, my compadres had not. Poems poured forth into issue after issue of *The World*. But I was glad to see that I was not the only poet to question poetry either. Why write? is a question that writers often ask themselves. It is also a question that critics ask of writing. Specifically, why write poetry? Was it really where news stayed news or because people died every day for a lack of what was found there?

How important was poetry to the East Village or, for that matter, the 1960s? I would say that poetry was an essential art of the Sixties, as it was particularly important to a place like the East Village, without which there was nothing but the nonlinear utterance, the scream, the shout, the grunt, the sigh. Without poetry, it seemed as if life was not worth living. I don't mean that as an exaggeration but as a simple fact. I was too poor to be a filmmaker, lacked physical space to paint. I did not have a facility with music, despite my second grade grammar school nun telling my parents that I had musical genius. So I had writing, something I had done since I was eight years old, something which I thought was an essential part of me, even knowing that writing was as illusory as anything else.

One of the most frightening experiences I had while at university was to take a psychedelic drug inadvertently, and the first thing that went was language. I found it terrifying to be in a world without language, without words, I should say, because there are many languages, of the hands, the heart, the eyes, etc. I meant the language of everyday speech, the common tongue, the vulgar tongue, a great luxury to everyone who wanted to avail themselves of its essence. I was one of those people. I craved words the way drug addicts craved a fix. If it was not going to be poetry, I thought, well, let it be prose.

This is what we call a luxury problem, though. As I walked the energetic streets of the downtown world, the rest of the world was imploding with violence, across the oceans in Southeast Asia and on the urban streets of America.

In the aftermath of the riots, the already radicalized poets and writers whom I knew in the East Village became even more radical. The Detroit poet Allen Van Newkirk published a one-page broadsheet with poems by Jones/ Baraka about the riots, with giant-sized 75-point Hobo type headlines which read:

POETRY IS REVOLUTION / REVOLUTION IS POETRY

In the next year, Van Newkirk would get a bunch of us to show our sympathies for the strikers at Columbia University by distributing another issue of his broadsheet in support of the revolutionary actions in Morningside Heights. Still later, Allen would convene a meeting of various poets, including myself, Andrei Codrescu, and Ron Edson, trying to draw us into an underground revolutionary cell that would take radical actions against the war, the riots, and other social injustices. I remember the flat in which we met was tiny and crammed with books, pamphlets, broadsheets, and, yes, even a cache of weapons. I realized that I was angry and felt revolutionary, and certainly I talked a good game, but I was not ready to be like the Weather Underground and their bomb-making factory in an exclusive brownstone off lower Fifth Avenue. I was a writer, a fighter, a talker, a drinker, a random drug user, a Catholic anarchist, politically non-violent but socially a bit more explosive than that. I boxed in little gyms on the Lower East Side, and tried to practice political non-violence, and was certainly via my Franciscan education antiwar. But I was not ready to become a revolutionary working underground for a cause whose shadowy edges I had no knowledge of. Besides, I had found a job through Joel Oppenheimer, working the six to midnight shift at the Eighth Street Bookshop in the Village, alongside Andrei and other young writers, where we talked the night away about books and other cultural matters.

One by one, Andrei, Ron, and myself, declined Allen Van Newkirk's offer to go underground and become true revolutionaries. I now see that moment as a turning point in my young life. There were many things about which I disagreed with my downtown fellows and revolutionaries. I liked the way things were; if not with the war and the domestic injustices still meted out to Black citizens, then I liked my aimless life of bohemian scruff and bother, these dirty, noisy, dangerous streets. I liked walking to the classes at the Old Courthouse. I liked engaging my friends in discussions of poetry and prose, of foreign films and baseball, tennis, basketball, but never boxing or football, all of which things we talked about at the bookshop in the Village.

So there was Allen Van Newkirk, who explained to us that we would therefore have to leave, and we did. I don't think I ever saw him again, nor have I seen his poetry published in small press magazines since that day. I often wonder what happened to him. He was a very good poet.

In my endless walk, it began to rain. It was a cold, raw night, and I came back towards the Poetry Project earlier than usual. When the workshops ended, I would come back to the Old Courthouse, open the front door, creep upstairs, and unfold a sleeping bag upon the workshop table. The place was dark and deserted and not just a little bit scary. I nipped into Joel's office where there was a beautiful roll top desk which he never used, and helped myself to his large bottle of whiskey, and then went to sleep in the other room. If I was dreaming of this one's eyes and that one's nose, another's longness, or one's compactness, I also dreamed of my songlines, how walking from place to place downtown was beginning to define who I was. I decided that night, before going off to sleep, that I was not a poet; I was a prose writer. In the morning, before going for my long walk from east to west across St. Marks Place and 8th Street into the Village, I sat down at the workshop table, and I began to write prose. I was there, only with prose instead of poetry. That is where I was—there—and that was good enough for now. I thought of that line from Frank O'Hara's poetry in which he said that even in his prose he was a poet.

In the autumn of 1967, I began to work as a clerk at the Eighth Street Bookshop. Joel Oppenheimer had provided my reference to the owner, Eli Wilentz, and I was hired. Because

I had no known address, I used Ron's or maybe even Joel's address to secure the job. The shop was a large bookstore— at least for its time it was a large one—located in the middle of West 8th Street between Fifth and Sixth avenues. There were three or four floors of books, and everyone in the Village, it seemed, stopped into the shop to browse. I worked from six to midnight six nights a week, and thought that I had died and gone to heaven. For a young writer to work in the Eighth Street Bookshop was comparable to a young painter apprenticing with Michelangelo or Titian, or put in more contemporary terms—with Mark Rothko or Philip Guston. Like City Lights in North Beach and the Grolier in Harvard Square, the Eighth Street Bookshop was not merely a bookstore; it was a literary establishment of people and ideas, and it was a destination in the Village. "Meet me at the Eighth Street Bookshop," she said, and you knew she was hip and with it, a reader and a writer, and someone who knew where things were at. It was the ideal job for a guy like me. I had likeminded people to talk to, I could buy books at a good discount, and after work, I could drink from midnight to four in the morning in the Village or the East Village bars, the best time to be in such places. In the mornings, I wrote, usually in a notebook because I could not afford a typewriter and my living conditions were too precarious to have possessions other than the clothes I wore and the bag I carried with my notebook, pens, and whatever book I was reading at the time.

Besides the books that were on the shelves and the

books being read and forever discussed behind the counter and out on the floor, there were the customers who regularly visited the Eighth Street Bookshop. Everyone who was anyone in the literary and cultural worlds had a charge account at the store, and to charge was not some impersonal credit card affair, but a clerk writing up every purchase: one sheet filed in the cash register, the other given to the customer. The regular charge customers included Edward Albee, Anais Nin, Donald Barthelme, Albert Murray, and several times a week—usually on his motorcycle, which he parked outside the store—the author and neurologist Oliver Sacks. The list of writers and celebrities whose charge accounts had been frozen was equally illustrious—a who's who of downtown cultural life.

One could namedrop all night mentioning the people who frequented the bookshop, including such Village locals as Djuna Barnes, author of *Nightwood*, who lived in a chic cul-de-sac around the corner. Toni Morrison, Erica Jong, Susan Sontag, and various downtown celebrities from Andy Warhol's Factory came by. Jazz musicians from Cecil Taylor to Nina Simone came in. So did Jimi Hendrix and Eric Clapton. Blustering, drunken celebrities wandered in—Paul Ford (of *Sergeant Bilko*), Jack Palance, and perhaps the most unusual of them all, one of the Gallos, a local Mafia superstar who lived across the street.

"I read a lot of Albert Camus," Gallo once told me,

perusing the fiction. A lifetime later I'd walk by Umberto's Clam Bar in Little Italy, and to whoever I was with I'd say, "Where one of the Gallos got whacked," as if my having talked to one of them in the bookshop on Eighth Street gave me a greater proximity to this hoodlum and his brother.

Nearly everyone I met in the bookshop, whether a clerk or customer, had an interest in literature. "Interest" is perhaps not the right word; most of these people were passionate about ideas, and obsessed by books and writers. Their love seemed almost erotic; they talked about reading a book the way someone else might speak of a love-conquest.

"I read all of my first volume of Proust over the weekend, not leaving the apartment once," a clerk would say.

Another clerk responded with: "I've been locked away with Madame Bovary for days."

Anais Nin had left a package behind when she visited the bookshop. She lived locally when she was in New York, and I was asked to get the package to her. As a result, we got into a brief correspondence, all of it long lost except one note she wrote me on TWA In-Flight stationary. Here is the letter in its entirety:

Dear Michael Stephens

Your letter pleased me and I was going to answer it

when I left unexpectedly to prepare a script for Jeanne Moreau—I liked that you feel like writing—for I never think of it as a task but a pleasure, which heightens and enhances my life and keeps me hearing the "beautiful voices," as you say. Yes sometimes one questions—locking oneself up in a room—but now I know it is one way to create your own world as one wishes it—So I hope you'll create yours—as you wish it.

Anais

She invited me to a party at the Gotham Bookmart for one of her book publications, and on another occasion, she invited me to dinner at her apartment with some friends of hers, but my date pulled out at the last moment, and I never managed to show up. Sometimes I imagine that the other guests would have been Henry Miller and Lawrence Durrell, in which case I screwed up grandly by not showing up to that dinner.

When we first came on our shift, the owner, Eli Wilentz—a small, neat, casual man with a Nat Sherman-like cigarillo stuck between his lips or burning between his fingertips—was finishing his business for the day and oversaw what was going on. Eli reminded me of an older Bob Dylan, his size and wan complexion and his face. Sometimes Wilentz's son Sean—now a well-known historian—and later a biographer of Bob Dylan!—was there, too. The former day manager was something of a downtown literary celebrity, a poet by the name of A. B. Spellman who, when he left the bookshop, became a prominent arts administrator. But he was also a good poet, very much in the style of Joel Oppenheimer, I thought, and he wrote a luminously elegant and simple prose, as evidenced by his classic work, *Four Lives in the Bebop Business* (1966).

The dramatic events about the Vietnam War and the inner city riots were sometimes masked by the quotidian activities of life in downtown Manhattan. I continued to sleep on the couches and floors of different friends' apartments; I went to the cheap movies in the afternoon. By six at night, I was back to work at the bookshop. The night shift was taken care of by the night manager Conrad and his assistant Dudley. Both were well-read and brimming with recommendations about what to read. They almost never agreed with each other, though. Conrad was far more patrician in his tastes; Dudley was more eclectic, more willing to contradict himself and— because he was a painter, I thought—more easygoing. Yet who could top Conrad for intellectual vigor? Andrei Codrescu, that's who. Though he had just turned twenty-one, Andrei's reading was quite extraordinary, and in many languages. He recommended that I read a wide range of poets from Andre Breton to Pablo Neruda. He spoke of Rimbaud as perhaps being the greatest poet ever (Codrescu thought so; so did Henry Miller; and so did

I). Certainly Arthur Rimbaud was the purest emotionally, having completed his major works in his late teens, whereupon he became a 19th-century gunrunner and revolutionary in Africa, a romantic's romantic. One night I heard Andrei shout: "Oxidize the gargoyles!" I learned later that he was quoting Rimbaud. Another time I heard Andrei say something to the effect: "The arctic honey blabbed thus causing darkness." When I asked him what he was talking about, he pointed to a poetry book on one of the bookshelves.

"John Ashbery," he said.

Another recommendation—perhaps the most durable Andrei made—was to read Jorge Luis Borges, starting with *Ficciones*, which Andrei thought of as a kind of sacred text for a young prose writer. Borges was the Argentine fabulist, miniaturist, and witty philosopher of time and prose. Andrei also recommended Paul Valery's novel *Monsieur Teste* and Huysmans's *Against Nature*, a book which Conrad, the night manager, also recommended. The Huysmans was filled with late 19th-century decadent prose, and Valery once wrote what became a lifelong writing belief for me: we do not finish writing a poem, only abandon it in despair.

Conrad had his own strict reading list that he drew up for me one evening shortly after I started working at the bookstore, during a lull in the usual crush of people buying books. He considered me to be hopelessly saturated in Irish literature (Joyce, Beckett, Yeats, O'Casey, Synge)—to him, I was steeped in Irish Catholicism and had come from a large immigrant and parochial family in Brooklyn—though Conrad did have some begrudging interest in James Joyce. I might be saved, he felt, by reading some European modernists. He told me to eschew James Joyce and Flann O'Brien and read the books on his list.

"Flann who?" I asked.

"O'Brien," he said, as if everyone knew the writer. "*At Swim-Two-Birds*."

Now I wasn't sure what he was talking about or even what language he was using, but fortunately O'Brien's comic masterpiece was in print and Conrad lent me a copy. This wonderfully funny book would go in and out of print throughout my life, proving that the fortunes of a book are not assured simply because it influences every writer who reads it.

But O'Brien was only a sidebar to the modernist reading list Conrad had in mind for me. Starting in the 19th century, when the novel reigned supreme, Conrad's list rushed into the 20th century, a Modernist express. There was no Borges, Beckett, Kafka, or Calvino on the list, and few women writers. (At the time, no women were employed in the bookshop either, although that was to change within a few short years.) The list was a literary equivalent to Conrad's interests in architecture— a solid house of a list for a sort of Nabokovian modernism.

Conrad's list included, in fact, several of Nabokov's

novels. But it also included Ford Madox Ford's *Good Soldier*, Wyndham Lewis's *Tarr*, Huysmans's *Against Nature*, Choderlos de Laclos's *Dangerous Liaisons*, Robert Musil's *Man without Qualities*, and some books by Gombrowicz, Lermontov, and a few others. Vladimir Nabokov I knew to be a great, living Russian emigre writer and author of *Lolita*, a best-selling novel at the time. Ford and Lewis, I would learn, were great English prose stylists from earlier in the century, and I certainly had heard their names from reading Ezra Pound's poetry.

As to the other names on Conrad's list, I would learn that J. K. Huysmans was a mid-19th-century bureaucrat who went on to write some of the most experimental fiction of that century. Robert Musil, an Austrian, was considered to be—at least in Middle Europe—the experimental equivalent of James Joyce or Virginia Woolf.

These literary lists of world literature aside, our world was quite insular. We were safely ensconced in our clerk's jobs in the well-run bookshop on West 8th Street. The Village was an old and cultured place, the customers who came into the shop well-educated and often renowned people. Nearly everyone was antiwar, pacificists, antiestablishment, and very left-leaning. The more radical members of the Poetry Project were involved in the Angry Arts, which was a grassroots organization that went off on a flat-bed truck, reading anti-war poems to different communities in the New York area. Many of the clerks, myself included, were deeply sympathetic to what happened to LeRoi Jones in Newark. During the recent riots, he was bashed in the head by a policeman, and then arrested for assaulting a cop. At his trial, the judge cited Jones/Baraka's poetry as the incitement for the Newark riots. Besides reading and discussing books and making lists, the clerks were talking about the war and the riots.

A customer came into the bookshop asking for the Proust biography.

"Painter?" Conrad asked.

"No, Marcel Proust," the man said. "He was a French writer."

"I mean the Painter biography," Conrad said, not losing a beat, and break from his stony countenance.

"Obviously you didn't hear me," the customer said, ever more annoyed. "I don't want the biography of the painter Marcel Proust but of the writer Marcel Proust."

Conrad walked away from him and came back with Maurice Painter's biography of Marcel Proust while the customer held the book in hand, without noting the author's last name and repeated, "Yes, yes, this is it, the biography of the writer."

Another time a customer could not think of the title of a book she was looking for. Charles Dudley walked to the back of the shop, and came back with a best-selling book on memory.

"Wow, man, how did you figure that out?" Andrei asked.

"A wild guess," Dudley said.

Dudley and Conrad's tastes in books were as different as their physical appearances. Conrad's neat, casual ivy league look—pressed khakis, blue oxford button-down shirt, dirty bucks, horned-rim glasses—stood in contrast to Dudley's lumberjack shirts and rawhide vests, and his corncob pipe. Conrad had a downtown New York accent, although certain words betrayed his upbringing in Bedford-Stuyvesant, Brooklyn, not far from where I grew up. Dudley's accent was Down East, decidedly from Maine, New England, the country.

It was Dudley who first recommended that I read Gabriel Garcia Marquez's *One Hundred Years of Solitude*, arguably the most influential novel of the late twentieth century. I recall reading the novel in two or three sittings. Then came the discussion of the book, usually during slow periods in the evening when not too many customers were lined up at the counter to buy books.

Dudley loved the book, saying it was the best novel he had ever read. Conrad could barely tolerate it. He pointed to a fast-selling novel by Toni Morrison, and he said, "Toni was begat by Gabriel and he was begat by William Faulkner and—"looking to me, "Irish will tell you who Willie was begat by."

"James Joyce," I said, tentatively.

"Exactly," he said.

"But who is Joyce begat by?" one of the clerks asked.

"Time to work," Conrad said as a parade of customers came marching in.

Conrad was reputed to have known, perhaps even to have been a personal friend of, Vladimir Nabokov. Had Conrad studied with Nabokov at Cornell? No, Conrad told me that he was a dropout from the University of Michigan, not Cornell. But Conrad did not elaborate. It was said, around the bookshop, that they had once been friends but had a falling-out. Another rumor was that Conrad had written the introduction to Nabokov's first published novel in America, a book that came out from New Directions but that was out-of-print at the time. Perhaps it was that essay which led to their detachment from one another. Or maybe this was one of those Village rumors with no basis in fact, a bit like Joe Gould's history of the world in multiple volumes, whereas the work existed nowhere but in Joe Gould's mind.

It was clear to me, observing Conrad, that he was a type of intellectual with which I was not familiar: he was not a writer or an academic. With the exception of a few bookshop cognoscenti with whom he talked, his intelligence seemed strictly a private matter, existing for its own sake. Conrad's reading—and his breadth of literary knowledge— had nothing to do with acquiring academic promotions or pedantry to feed a shaky writer's ego. It was a kind of pure intelligence; he was a person who loved books for their own sake.

A woman came into the bookshop one evening. She was writing her dissertation on Vladimir Nabokov, and she asked Conrad if he was the person who wrote the introduction to the New Directions novel. He looked her straight in the eye and said, "No, I'm not," and walked away. When I asked him about it later in the evening, he said, "It's a long story," and once again walked away.

Many years later, browsing a bookstall on Broadway near Columbia University, I came across that Nabokov novel. Conrad had indeed written the introduction.

No formal education ever quite equaled the informal one I received working at the Eighth Street Bookshop. The ideas found in books were discussed so fervently and yet thrown about so casually; the discussions were intermittent, between customers, but they were intense and deep, full of loving detail for literature and the art of reading. What I acquired was not a set of literary categories or methods of analysis or substantive insights about specific books. Something more fundamental occurred, and it was vastly more precious: a full-body immersion in the world of writing, for six hours every night, six days a week, from poets, prose writers, autodidacts, pedants, bibliophiles, and mere shop clerks (probably the most brilliant of all the observers). They would pullulate and whinge, become ecstatic, even begin to shout and point their fingers into your chest as they emphasized how important a certain book or author was. I never seemed to take offense at this passionate intensity, but rather wrote down what they told me I should be reading, and then went straight away to conduct that reading assignment.

My reading was thought adequate by the overly well-read clerks and management. Some of them thought I read far too much contemporary American poetry—especially William Carlos Williams. Ezra Pound, though his politics were deemed deplorable, was considered an acceptable stylistic influence. His anti-Semitism and his siding with Mussolini during World War II, not to mention his anti-American speeches on Italian radio, were all reasons to vilify Pound. But the brilliance of the ideas and writing style in his *Cantos* was reason enough to read Pound, albeit with a grain of salt. Neither Pound nor Williams was the poet of choice for the Eighth Street Bookshop crew, though. They preferred Neruda, Vallejo, Montale, Celan, and Cavafy—writers who were South American or European, not provincially North American. Others dismissed all poets as literary elves, with the exception of Mandelstam and Akmatova.

Disagreements in the bookshop were not always civil. A red-haired Cuban refugee used to take offense at nearly everything I uttered, finding me unrefined, unlettered, vulgar, and a bore. He would say this to me or others he did not like: "You are so boring and dull." The only person he seemed to tolerate was Andrei, who sympathized with his Castro-centered leftist Cuban politics, which is not to suggest that anyone in the bookshop was anything but left of Che—it was the height of the Vietnam War, and Greenwich Village and the Lower East Side were right there at fever-pitch center of the anti-war movement. Every weekend we would see the Village short story writer Grace Paley and friends in front of the Women's House of Detention on Sixth Avenue across from 8th Street, protesting the war with signs and banners.

One evening during this period I ran into Sam Abrams on Second Avenue back in the East Village, and he told me that he was going to be late for the workshop. Would it be possible to open the Old Courthouse? I said I could do that for him as it was my day off from working at the bookshop. We went to his long, narrow apartment which was directly across from St. Mark's Church. Sam, besides his poetry writing and teaching, was very active in radical politics. A Classics scholar, his Rolodex was gigantic, containing the names of every indictable leftwing activist downtown. He was a pot-head, as his later poetry books eminently showed, and he constantly smoked dope. This often made him forgetful, so he fumbled around for the key to the Courthouse door.

"Barbara, where are the fucking keys?" he shouted to his wife down the hall.

His two young sons zoomed around the flat, playing a game.

Chaos theory was a reality at Sam's.

"Look in your fucking pocket, Sam."

He did.

The keys were there.

Sam said, quoting Joel Oppenheimer, who in turn was quoting Ezra Pound, who in turn was quoting Confucius: "The way out is via the door. Why is it that no one will avail themselves of it?"

He handed me the keys, and I quickly made a copy of them, which I presumed Sam understood I would do. With the new set, I now had access to the Old Courthouse out of hours, and therefore a place to sleep, inside the workshop room when no one was there. I was technically speaking no longer homeless. So that is how I began living at the Old Courthouse in the autumn of 1967. I stowed my sleeping bag in Joel's office, in one of the drawers of his big rolltop desk because he was rarely around and, if he was, he never went into the office. But like all alkies, he had hidden some bottles in case of an emergency, so I began to drink from them to keep warm at night when the heat was turned off in the Old Courthouse.

I told Sam what I had done, once I gave back his set of keys, but he was the kind of person who would not object to such ingenuity. It appealed to his deepest anarchist nature. He liked that I was living by my wits out on the street.

IV.

THE FAILURE ARTIST

"Although the individuals you'll meet in these pages, the writers, will separate themselves as the years go by, what you have before you is really the expression of a small society, a literary commune."

—Seymour Krim

It was my day off from the bookshop, and it was raining. I had not been attending the writing workshops because of my job's six to midnight schedule. Before the rain came, I had been walking all day everywhere, trying to figure out a way to improve my life. My latest dive was the Old Courthouse, in the very room where the workshops took place. I would circle back home after the writing workshops wound down. When they ended, I got to go home. The rain was relentless, and I was soaked through from the downpour, and so I headed back to the Old Courthouse and went upstairs a bit earlier than usual. A writing workshop was still in session, as I slipped into the room and sat down in the back away from the workshop table. The room was full of writers, not young ones but people in their late twenties and thirties and older. The class seemed more focused and reasoned than the poetry workshop which could get adolescently peevish when someone's feelings got hurt over Joel's criticism of their poetry. I soon discovered that this was the prose workshop, and the teacher at the front of the room, an older man in thick black glasses, a denim work-shirt, floral print tie, corduroy jacket, and jeans with shiny brown loafers was Seymour Krim, the essayist, editor, and downtown gadfly public intellectual. People called him Krim or Seymour or Sy, and he was more moderator than officious workshop coordinator. The opinions were flowing fast and furiously, one person after another unloading their responses about a piece of writing, though backing up their reactions by referring to the text, pointing out, in the language of writing workshops, what worked and what didn't work. I knew about Krim, but only slightly, as I had read his only book of essays several years earlier when an older writer who was his friend gave me a copy of *Views of a Nearsighted Cannoneer* (1961).

The writing workshop was meeting in what amounted to my bedroom when there were no classes in the building. When no one was there, I got my sleeping bag out of Joel's office, which he no longer used very much. I was not exactly mentally fit or even a little well. I had gone from living at the edge to living in some kind of pit—a rut in which I had put up curtains.

My boots leaked, my feet were cold, and my body shivered, my long hair dripping over my shoulders and down my back. I probably looked like a tramp off the Bowery, one block west of the workshop. I shivered inside of a long, heavy military overcoat. Luckily on the Lower East Side, I did not appear that unusual, just another bug-eyed, long-haired, underpaid and under-appreciated bookstore clerk and poet. The people in the workshop took no notice of me, as they were engaged in critiquing a story. This was prior to the age of Xerox copies being handed out the week before, and it was long before email attachments. A writer showed up with one copy, not necessarily typed, and read from it; sometimes the piece was passed around, not to be read in its entirety, but perused for parts that either piqued one's interest or raised red flags about its problems. It was also before cigarette smoking was banned in public spaces, so the room was thick with smoke, and the ashtrays (old coffee cans) on the table were piled high with butts. Some of the people in the class were drinking cans of beer, a nice touch, I thought. It being the East Village, marijuana scented the air.

The rain had introduced a dampness into the room that was not going away just because I or anyone else had gotten out of the downpour. There was a kind of wet-dog damp to the people, place, and even their manuscripts.

I cannot explain why, but I felt immediately at ease in this group, even at home with them. What they were saying about the piece of writing, even though I hadn't heard it being read, rang true for me as critical response. They spoke about the characters, the storyline, the mood of the piece, the language, and, like the poetry workshop, the voice of the writer or, in this case, the narrator. Was it an unreliable narrator or just the writer fumbling for a point-of-view? They spoke about what worked and what didn't work, about epiphanies or lack thereof, even about that Henry Jamesian thing, "the felt experience." (I imagined a red dinner jacket worn by Oscar Wilde!) What they were talking about—prose—interested me. Most of the thousands of notebooks I had filled up since I was a small boy were piled high with prose, even if a good amount of the notebooks still included poetry. I had written on the stoops of my family's houses in Brooklyn and out on Long Island. I had filled countless notebooks with prose when I worked on the ship in the Mediterranean in 1965, what seemed like a lifetime away, but was only two years ago.

After the class ended, I managed to disappear into the Old Courthouse, like the Phantom of the Opera, and when they were gone, I backtracked upstairs again to the workshop room, writing all night in my notebook. I managed to complete a story by daybreak, worked on it through the week and then brought it to the workshop. A part of me—a very cocky part—kept telling myself that I could write as well as or even better than what I had heard as the workshop progressed into the evening. From the week before, I learned immediately that they were a critical group, tearing things apart, and I would be no exception. They roughed me up, but I was able to take it, and after the class, Krim asked me if I would not mind getting the piece revised and back to him, typed and ready to be submitted, as he was a contributing editor at *Evergreen Review*, the downtown but international literary magazine published by Grove Press. I had been reading *Evergreen Review* since I was a fifteen-year-old runaway, and it is where I first encountered Jean Genet, Robert Gover and John Rechy. I still didn't have a typewriter, but I knew enough people who did, and I got it typed up and re-submitted to Seymour before the next class.

During that next class, I read another story I had written and worked on through the week, and again Krim asked me to type it up. He also was working with *Provincetown Review*, trying to get it revived, and he wanted to show them this new story. *Provincetown Review* had famously published parts of Hubert Selby's *Last Exit to Brooklyn* in the early 1960s, and there had been a trial for obscenity. Selby was my favorite author, and his novel was the most important book in my young life.

Week after week that autumn, I attended the prose workshop on my day off from the Eighth Street Bookshop.

I had been careful not to tell Krim or any of the others about my situation, and how I was living illegally in the Old Courthouse. I was worried that Krim would ask me to hand back the keys. But it did slip out one evening, and it got back to Seymour, and instead of castigating me, he expressed his alarm for me.

"Can you survive this way?" he asked.

"I can," I said.

"How?"

"This is an improvement over how I was living."

"Oh, shit," Krim said, astonished at my situation.

At the time of first attending the prose writing workshop at St. Mark's, I only knew Seymour Krim's work cursorily. Now I re-read his essay in *The Beats* (1960), and a few other things I came across in the underground newspapers he wrote for occasionally. Years earlier, I had read the small-press version of his first and so far only book, *Views of a Nearsighted Cannoneer*, and was impressed by the style, though I had long forgotten exactly what its content was. Like all the other young writers at the Poetry Project, I was self-absorbed, self-involved, self-obsessed, and more interested in my own writing than anyone else's, including a teacher's writings. In fact, seeing Krim, in his denim shirts and floral ties, his corduroy jackets with his ironed jeans and his polished loafers, I thought he was a bit of a dufus, and everyone else in the workshop seemed to regard him in a way that was poised between contempt and admiration. In many respects, he and I were studies in opposites. I was living on the street and he was living in a flat on East 10th Street. I was preparing for the revolution and he thought of himself as a downtown intellectual, not even a radical. He listened to classical music, and still went to uptown literary cocktail parties. But Krim's saving graces were many, too. He smoked marijuana profusely (not impressive to me, but to the class); he was certifiably *nuts* (his words, not mine); he was a great booster of everyone's writings, a kind of literary cheerleader, willing to take a backseat to our own glory; he was kind and compassionate, even if occasionally a pain in the ass and a bit of a yenta when it came to worrying and kvetching. Of course, his moods came on like the tides, and then his bipolar side took hold, all bets off, the insults or slights magnifying, his towards us, and his perceived grievance of us towards him.

Sometimes, now that I knew Krim, walking down Second Avenue, I ran into him. He invited me to his apartment, a studio space so cramped with books and records, you couldn't even move once you sat down in a chair. We smoked marijuana and then we both became unusually paranoid until I ran out the door, demons chasing me across Second Avenue, one hundred feet from his doorstep. Pot was never my drug of choice. Marijuana brought out the worst in me (paranoia and distrust); it rarely was spiritual and transcendent, the way others described the experience.

When Joel Oppenheimer looked about for a new person to fill the prose boots at the Poetry Project, he didn't have to go beyond 10th Street to find his prose-writing teacher. Seymour lived across from St. Mark's Church in that quaint row of older buildings from a by-gone era. As good a writer as he was, he probably was an even better teacher. Krim had already been teaching for a bit at Columbia University and elsewhere, so this was not virgin territory for him, and he was, I would soon learn, a natural as a teacher. Certainly he and Joel were the two teachers I most admired at that time. In their different ways, Joel and Seymour reminded me of a Krim essay about his own mentors, entitled "Two Teachers—Nuts, Two Human Beings!" which was the last piece in the reissue of his *Cannoneer* essays around the time when I first met Krim in 1967. Joel Oppenheimer saw me as a good poet while Krim perceived of me as a potentially great prose writer, so naturally I levitated towards the prose workshop with even more enthusiasm than I brought to Joel's poetry workshop the year before.

If having a fiction workshop at the St. Mark's in the Bowery Poetry Project wasn't oxymoronic enough ("it was, after all, a POETRY project," Ron Padgett once said to me when I asked him, years later, why the prose-writing workshop was not as well-known as the poetry workshop), the class was taught by a nonfiction writer. Seymour Krim's only publication to date was that essay collection, originally published at the top of the 1960s, and then reissued seven years later by E. P. Dutton as a quality paperback. But who was this prose writer among the poets? Krim had worked as an editor for a range of newspapers and magazines, often at the fringes of the literary establishment, i.e., reviewing for *Commentary* and *Partisan Review*, but never anyone's darling. If Joel Oppenheimer was famously, as he said, everyone's second choice, Krim was their third, proof being that he was preceded at the prose workshop by Ishmael Reed and Steve Cannon. But he did have certain advantages to make him the next person in line to teach the class. His pedigree was tied to the Beats, rightly or wrongly, because of that eponymous anthology he had edited. He was a local East Village / Lower East Side author. Like so many other alternative writers, Krim had hung his hat with the outsiders and the experimenters, the wild and unrestrained, proclaiming himself a kindred spirit in essay after essay. Lastly and maybe even most important of all, he lived across the street from St. Mark's Church in-the-Bowery.

Running a prose workshop at a place called the Poetry Project must have appealed to Seymour's sense of the absurd. That a nonfiction writer would become the mentor to a new generation of fiction writers was equally ridiculous, and yet somehow just right. At any rate, what Ishmael Reed and Steve Cannon had done—teach the prose workshop to the unruly and unwashed Lower East Siders at the Poetry Project—Krim now began to do too. Having accepted the teaching position, Krim was offering classes in prose writing to the disaffected youths of the Lower East Side, some of them bald and pot-bellied and slouching towards middle age. Prose at the Poetry Project began with far less fanfare than poetry did. Yet almost immediately the prose workshop attracted a core of dedicated, serious writers. Jerry Jerome (Jerry Roth back then) remembers Ishmael Reed running the workshops at first, but very quickly getting into other activities, such as writing for the *East Village Other*, and so going off. Clark Whelton, who went on to have a career in the world of New York political journalism, observed that "I was disappointed when Ishmael left, but Krim brought something new that worked on a different level."

Krim's students from the Poetry Project read like a Who's Who of intellectual prominence on the Lower East Side circa 1967. There were, at various times, already published writers like John Bart Gerald and Bill Amidon, and a hard core of short story writers like George Blecher and Rascha Levinson, who were beginning to be published in literary magazines. At various times in its early days, writers such as Shulamith Firestone—author of *The Dialectic of Sex* (1970), one of the most important books in the feminist movement of that time—would turn up for a while. The African American novelist George Cain presented to the workshop some early drafts of his novel *Blueschild Baby* (1970). The semiotician Marshall Blonsky attended the workshop regularly, and so did the later two-time Academy Award-winning director Sarah Kernochan, who had been sent to the workshops by her teacher Grace Paley, while Sarah was still a student at Sarah Lawrence in Bronxville, New York. The pulp fiction writer Jerry Roth attended the workshop, and regular guests included Alan Kapelner, Ishmael Reed (the original workshop leader), and Donald Phelps, who, like Krim, was one of the really great essayists of the 1960s.

Seymour Krim was born in 1922, and grew up in New York on the Upper West Side. But at an early age (eight), Seymour's father died, and two years later, his mother committed suicide. In one of those *Cannoneer* essays, he put it this way: "My mother killed herself roof-wise just before I turned 10." In that same essay about Milton Klonsky, Krim's mentor and friend, he went on to write about his sheltered upbringing, encompassing the

Upper West Side, prep school in the suburbs, and camp in Maine, all of it liberally Jewish. Though orphaned early in his life, Krim managed to flourish under the guidance of older relatives. Still, the loss of his parents was to mark his entire life, making him identify deeply with the outsider, whether they were Black or white (his *Cannoneer* essay "Ask for a White Cadillac"), Jews or Gentiles (the essay "Be a Good Eli"), queer or straight ("Revolt of the Homosexual"), insane or "normal" ("The Insanity Bit"), the lover of life (Whitman particularly was an influence on Seymour in "Whitman at Home; Whitman and His Critics") or the suicide (his mother in the 1930s and chronicled in "Suicide in Toyland"). Krim himself would commit suicide in 1989, although under very different circumstances than his mother's. His own death was well planned out, including counseling, and it had to do not so much with despair at life but of an acceptance of life as it was, including an endpoint.

From the late 1940s and throughout the 1950s, he wrote for what were then considered traditional, Jewish intellectual journals, the kind of magazines that championed Saul Bellow and later Philip Roth. In the first essay in *Views of a Nearsighted Cannoneer*, Krim wrote of this intellectual journey that he was set upon early in his writing career. In that same essay, Krim states that it was American literature he wanted to write. Then something happened to him. He moved beyond the axis of Hemingway-Wolfe-Dreiser-Faulkner, and found another kind of voicing. He was placed in the impossible position, as he put it, of writing something that was emotionally real, and relate it to what he called "the interplanetary discussion," high on weed (tea, he called it), sitting in Ratner's cafeteria deli on Second Avenue, a few blocks from his apartment on 10th Street, at 3 AM.

Besides becoming less provincial and more internationalized, Krim became hipper, more aware of his immediate downtown surroundings. He anthologized writers such as Jack Kerouac, Gregory Corso, William Burroughs, Hubert Selby, Jr., Gary Snyder, and Allen Ginsberg, but also presented writers such as Norman Podhoretz, Herbert Gold, and Anatole Broyard, more nonfictional and critical voices, not so much alternative as in-the-know, even know-it-all in their breadth of literary knowledge. Yet Krim really straddled two worlds in his literary life—the hip downtown artist/writer world in which he lived and even flourished, and the more staid, establishment world of the *Partisan* and *Commentary* crowds. Krim's mentor Milton Klonsky easily moved between these two worlds—a friend of Delmore Schwartz and W. H. Auden, on the one hand, and, on the other, a friend to Seymour Krim and Anatole Broyard, who then owned a bookshop in the Village, and had not yet become a literary critic at the *New York Times*.

Ironically, Milton Klonsky, unlike Krim, opposed the idea of the singular voice shouting I, I, I, I. "Who were all these braided, pompous, regimental I's identified with me?" As was true with all of Krim's relationships, his friendship with Klonsky was competitive and edgy at times. Linearity is what created any semblance of order. Here is Krim answering his mentor, almost like a jazz trombone answering the saxophone solo which just preceded it. Klonsky wrote about this god above, not Krim's god which was, as he said, *"the god of life who thumps within my chest for more, faster, bigger, conquests for me, me, Me!"* [Italics are Krim's.] A theme and variation concerning the "I" in literature is offered by Joan Didion, who exemplified what Krim was getting at. In her essay/ speech, "Why I Write," in which she observes:

I

I

I

In many ways writing is the act of saying *I*, of imposing oneself upon other people, of saying *listen to me, see it my way, change your mind*. It's an aggressive, even a hostile act...

Krim's friend Dan Wakefield also has an essay riffing on the use of the first person singular and, for that matter, so does Henry David Thoreau, and certainly Krim's own literary hero Walt Whitman was not opposed to using the first person singular. But I am specifically making a reference to Krim and Klonsky, their relationship, their friendship, and how this I, I, I, this first person singular, imposed itself upon that interaction, and how it was both the glue which held them together and a further tension, their ungluing, if you will. By tension, I don't mean a negative impulse, but rather a human energy, as in the idea of tension being a component of all great art, whether visual, sonic or literary.

In his first book of essays, Krim admits that he wanted to be a fiction writer. In 1961 when *Views of a Nearsighted Cannoneer* came out, it was only 128 pages long. Six years later, E. P. Dutton published an expanded version of the essays as a quality paperback, and it was twice as long as the original book. He explained that the first publisher was tight for money, so he asked Krim to cut the Klonsky piece. In the expanded version of *Cannoneer*, Krim explains that the essays were written from 1957 to 1960, and it was his break-through work. Krim actually weaved bits of fiction throughout the essays, the reason being that "all the passionate floundering discussed in 'What's *This* Cat's Story?' is visible, tangible, on the page." He would go on to say that the entire book now added up to a story "—of the mind, of doubt, of writing, of ambition and certainly of one individual American over these last twenty years—as well as a set of statements. You decide."

Both George Orwell and Seymour Krim were sublime essayists, and shared affinities with failure. Orwell even concluded that "every book is a failure." One of Krim's best essays was entitled "For My Brothers and Sisters in the Failure Business," which, appropriately enough, concluded the last book he would publish while still alive. Of course, failure is an important, even a major and indispensable theme to serious nonfiction writers, people like Orwell, and even Krim to some extent, being the paradigms. The privileged Virginia Woolf's nonfiction blossoms with her acknowledged failures, and both she and Krim were suicides, a kind of ultimate gesture of the failed, as witness Sylvia Plath or Primo Levi, although in the case of the latter, I still have my doubts that he did kill himself.

If one measures a writing teacher's worth by the number of publications by former students, then Seymour Krim was a master tutor—anything but a failure. The number of books, articles, stories, essays, and scholarly works by writers who frequented his workshop at the Poetry Project is impressive. Nearly every student who regularly attended his workshop eventually published a book or had an extended writing career in journalism. If one measures the teacher's own writing as a kind of yardstick of worth, then Krim again comes out well. He did not write and publish a lot of books, but what he did produce was solid and, more important, his writing ages well; it endures. Though he only published four collections of essays in his lifetime—no novels, poems, stories or plays (except for the fragmentary pieces of creative writing in his first essay collection)—nonetheless those essays were achievements; they broke new ground for how one wrote in this genre.

Krim the essayist was in rarefied company, as his peers were writers like Joan Didion, Tom Wolfe, Gay Talese, James Baldwin, Vivian Gornick, and Edward Hoagland. Like literary nonfiction's sainted eminence, George Orwell, Krim understood that to be a successful essayist one had to portray her or his own personal failures. In his classic essay, "Such, Such Were the Joys..." Orwell, sounding almost Krimlike, says: "I had no money, I was weak, I was ugly, I was unpopular, I had a chronic cough, I was cowardly, I smelt." But failure, for writers like George Orwell or Seymour Krim, often has another dimension, and here Orwell notes that "this sense of guilt and inevitable failure was balanced by something else: that is, the instinct to survive." Seymour Krim was nothing if not an instinctual survivor.

Of course, Krim never lost sight of the irony in the use of such a word as failure. Although he deleted this passage from the final version before his suicide in 1989, Krim originally wrote in his essay:

I don't know if my fellow visionaries will tolerate the word "failure" when members of their blood families, looking to them for money, status, some tangible outer sign of the golden inner constellations they claim to have traveled, fling this ancient curse on them. Perhaps they should not accept it in any sense and preserve the innocence that started them on a quest beyond materialism, petty achievement, the reduction of their many selves into one Kodak-pure white shirtfront on which a conventional medal can be pinned. Perhaps.

One of Krim's most harrowing confessions of failure—and ironically one of his best written pieces of writing—appeared in his Beat anthology, and later in his own first essay collection. The essay is entitled "The Insanity Bit" (1959) and it is quintessential Krim, covering his failures and triumphs, and finally his clinical breakdown, receiving electro-shock treatments for his depression. But even in that Beat atmosphere of downtown Manhattan, Krim would write that "my closest and most brilliant friends did not really understand, or were afraid to understand, the contemporary insanity bit." Not only is this essay Krim at his finest, retrospectively it would seem one of the best and earliest examples of New Journalism, one of Seymour's passions—to make the best journalism literature or, at least, literary nonfiction, what he later called "creative nonfiction" or "total imaginative writing." Though it is primarily read as a literary text, Krim's essay "The Insanity Bit" made observations into the world of psychiatry that are still probing and instructive today.

Krim was best as a personal essayist who, like the great novelists he so much admired and wanted to emulate, had the power to evoke strong feelings and emotions, giving them a literary shape, where in reality they were formless and empty. Nowhere is his writing more poignant than when he describes an attempted suicide, and how a moment of grace in the harsh world redeemed his life from that eternal cipher known as his failed life. He rented a room in a hotel in Newark, New Jersey, at that time an urban backwater across the Hudson River from New York City. After attempting suicide and having failed, Krim went to a Polish bar, lonely for company even in a singular moment of self-annihilation. Then he had an epiphany as illuminating as any offered by his literary heroes. He sees a Polish girl doing a life-affirming folk-dance. The essayist breaks into "loving sobs like prayers. The sun of life blazed from her into my grateful heart." He goes back to his hotel room which suddenly has become "beautiful," and flushes the pills of his own annihilation down the toilet bowl. He writes: "The next morning I returned to Manhattan a chastened man, shaking my head at how close I had come to non-being."

A great teacher needs great students, and Seymour Krim found that in the prose workshop at the Poetry Project. Jane Mushabac, who attended the prose workshop regularly, would go on to a literary and academic career, publishing a history of New York City and a study entitled *Melville's Humor* (1981), as well as dramatic and performance pieces for the actress Tovah Feldshuh. Later, she became a professor at the City University of New York. She remembers her Monday night writing workshops in the 1960s being spent "in a room so bare and worn-looking it was perfect, nothing mattered but the writing and the writers. I climbed through the second floor window one time when we couldn't get in through the front door."

"I regularly got into the workshop room by climbing through that second floor window," I told Jane but I don't think that she believed me or knew exactly what I was talking about. But when I left my keys behind in that room and went out the door, the only way back into the building was to shinny up a drain pipe and lean precipitously over to the window, which once opened, allowed me entry into the room. My novel *Still Life* (1978) revisits this shinnying to the second floor window at the Old Courthouse; the book was illustrated with stills from Buster Keaton's life and movies. The performance artist Jill Kroesen printed the book herself after I showed her the mock-up I put together of how the novel should be illustrated.

Sometimes the key to the front door would get stuck and the door would not open, so I had to devise another method for getting in and out of the building.

But we were already on to other topics. Jane was remembering things from the earliest workshops, before I had showed up that rainy, cold night in November 1967.

"Seymour brought guest writers to sit in and talk about their work," she told me. "Once he brought a writer who stuttered. It was shocking but interesting that the men in the group accused this man, told him his stuttering was a form of aggression. That was typical; there was always this jockeying and aggression, in fact we wondered why Seymour would subject any writer friend to it, but he did, quite often. It was surprising, but ultimately liberating. No one was an authority. No one was at a different level.

Paddy Chayevsky came once and complained stingingly, if I remember correctly, about how Hollywood wrecked his book in making a movie about it. Aggression and criticism were pointed and yet not bitter, and they never stuck in the craw. That was invaluable. It was a balanced group too, lots of laughter."

Despite this warning of the criticism being too trenchant at times, I never felt intimidated, and I never looked back either.

One night, walking to the workshop, I ran into Clark Whelton, another workshop writer, and he was jacked up on the idea that we were actually in the present tense as we walked to the Old Courthouse south along Second Avenue. Clark was a big man, tall and seemingly athletic, like a former basketball player, though I don't know if he was athletic or ever played basketball. He grabbed me by the shoulders and shook me to attention. "Here we are, Stephens, this ain't no rehearsal. This is the real deal; this is it. We are alive in the present, no matter what we do with this life later in our writing. The writing is the after-thought, not the present moment, which is everything. We're alive, Stephens, we are part of this world of downtown New York, in the autumn of 1967." I could not have agreed with Clark more, nor did I ever find myself any closer to him as I did at that moment. We were walking past an Italian funeral parlor, and a coffin was being carried out to the curb and then slid into the back of a hearse. But Clark and I were alive, and we were well.

We were alive and this moment, whatever it was, it was significant to both of us. We entered the Old Courthouse in this heightened state of awareness, not drugged up, more jacked up on life, its spirit, and what we intended to do as writers to capture that moment. Clark would go on to write on politics for *The Village Voice*, and then several years later, to become a speechwriter for Ed Koch and later Rudy Giuliani, two well-known former New York mayors. I would go off in a very different direction.

Several years after that moment we shared walking down Second Avenue, Clark got me a job selling Christmas trees at East 4th Street and First Avenue. I had the midnight to eight in the morning shift, and I lasted there almost until Christmas when a gang pulled up with a couple of station wagons and began stuffing trees into the back of their cars. There were several of them, and they meant business, and I did not see myself dying to save the Christmas tree business. When the owner came in to work around eight that morning, I told him what happened, and he fired me on the spot. But not before I got paid for the work I had done.

Clark originally came to the class on the recommendation of a friend, liked what he heard and saw, and so became a regular.

"I got here to the Lower East Side in March of 1966, and by June I was flat broke, with a wife, daughter, and another one on the way."

This was a few months before he started to write

regularly for *The Village Voice* newspaper, everyone's downtown gazette, if for nothing else than Jules Feiffer's cartoons, which I considered pure genius. Clark wasn't really into writing fiction, though he did try his hand at it. He wanted to write nonfiction, and in many respects he had found the perfect writing workshop with a character like Seymour Krim at the helm.

Through most of the 1970s, Clark would work for *The Voice*, but as early as late 1967, he was publishing pieces there intermittently. After he left the newspaper in 1977, he worked as a speech writer for Ed Koch, when he took office as the mayor of New York City in 1978. He worked for Koch for twelve years, then for New York State Governor Mario Cuomo for five years. Clark rounded this out with two years working for Rudolph Giuliani, one of New York's more famous—and later controversial—mayors after 9/11, and years later, as President Donald Trump's consigliere. Whelton continued to work on political campaigns until a few years ago, when he retired, and now writes for himself full time. As for his involvement in the Poetry Project, it began with his attending workshops at the film division of the arts project, and it ended up with his attending Krim's workshop, which was where the two of us were heading when he told me this information in the enlightened register of a Bodhisattva.

Though marginalized as a writer for most of his life, Seymour Krim nonetheless knew all the big literary players, from Norman Mailer to James Baldwin, James Jones to Mario Puzo, as well as the sharpest critical minds who would set the standards for his generation, including Norman Podhoretz, Milton Klonsky, and Anatole Broyard. But Krim confessed, despite his being editor of *The Beats*, that he "met Kerouac only twice, both for brief periods of not more than 15 minutes, and communication between us was abrupt and unreal." Yet because Krim was the editor of that anthology, he would forever be associated with Kerouac, Ginsberg, Burroughs, Corso, and all the other Beat writers until the end of his days. Sometimes Krim's affinities with these outsider writers among the Beats matched up well with his own sensibility. In an interview, Allen Ginsberg talks about Kerouac in a way that reminds me of Krim's writing, both in its description and in its rhythms: "... his craft is the perfect executive conjunction of archetypal memorial images articulating present observation of detail and childhood epiphany fact." Wow! That is one fucking good sentence by Ginsberg. Like Kerouac, who was known to coin memorable phrases such as *The Beats*, *Naked Lunch*, *bop prosody*, etc., Seymour Krim was also good with names and labels.

One of the essays in *Cannoneer* is entitled "Making It!" This essay is a jazzy, manic shout about the virtues of ambition in a city like New York. Krim did not coin the phrase "making it," but he was the first writer to use it in a literary context, to show it as a kind of writer's unstated ambition. Yet Krim, the outsider, a marginalized writer, this bottom dog of literature, the quintessential failure artist, could also be the person scripting the good lines for everyone else, though somehow never being acknowledged for it. Ten years after Krim wrote and published his essay called "Making It!" (1958), Norman Podhoretz published a splashy memoir called (what else?) *Making It* (1968). This pattern of pilfering Seymour for his ideas and phrases would plague his life from beginning until its end. The editor of Krim's selected essays, *What's This Cat's Story*? notes that Krim also coined the phrase "radical chic" in his essay, "Who's Afraid of *The New Yorker* Now?" Yet Tom Wolfe would co-opt the phrase as his own almost immediately afterward. And while Krim did not coin the phrase "creative nonfiction," he was the person for whom the expression was invented when he taught a class in literary nonfiction in the creative writing program for undergraduates at Columbia University's School of General Studies up in Morningside Heights on the Upper West Side of Manhattan. I understand now that other writers may have also used the term "creative nonfiction," but Krim's use of it at Columbia was the earliest I had heard the term. As I noted, the phrase that Krim preferred to use was "total imaginative writing."

The idea of time being in a continuum of one tense is an important one in terms of Seymour Krim's development as a writer of nonfiction prose, a writer of his time, the present tense in post-war America, particularly in downtown Manhattan. But how Krim affected this one-tense universe was different from all his contemporaries, especially the literary ones. Using fiction as his paradigm, he nonetheless went in search of a nonfiction writer's Holy Grail. Krim said: "I believe there is agreement that serious fiction in our century has tried to get closer than previously to literal experience in both its technique and exact autobiographical detail." This has to do with something Krim observed in his own Klonsky essay, and that is to "come up with an answer as tough as the truth." In that same essay, Krim quotes his mentor as saying that "the poet must think with nothing less than the mind of God."

One could say that Krim's relationship was not to God or Joe Gould, but to failure, shunning it, on the one hand ("Making It!"), and embracing it, on the other ("The Insanity Bit" or "For My Brothers and Sisters in the Failure Business"). In between these poles of human existence, there were the more level-headed things in life, like reading and writing. Reading and writing were two ways to exist meaningfully. After the Second World War, Anatole Broyard opened a Village bookstore, an undertaking which he said was as romantic as "living off the land or sailing around the world." People like Broyard, Klonsky, and Krim "didn't simply read books," Broyard said. "We became them."

The young Seymour Krim is so rapturous about Milton Klonsky that before meeting him in 1945, he refers to that year as "medieval," meaning, I think, that Seymour's young intellectual life was still in the dark ages of its development. Curiously, the third person in this troika, Anatole Broyard, dwelt upon this time after the war with an equal amount of exuberance and optimism. "Nineteen forty-six was a good time—perhaps the best time—in the twentieth century." One can imagine—even if *one* had just been born in 1946 as I had—how good the times must have been, the war ended, America a nation of great potential for young writers and intellectuals like Krim, Klonsky, or Broyard. It was Anatole Broyard, of these three, who noted that when he looked back on his own life—his memoir was written just before he died—he was amazed by his "original capacity to believe." It was in that year, 1946, when Krim and Klonsky were new friends that Anatole Broyard noted that "for the first time, we existed."

This idea of existing would remain an issue in all of Seymour Krim's own essays, and if he existed, was he worth anything, did his existence have any value? Why was he here, for what purpose? Did his own writing amount to anything other than scratchings on the page? Was writing itself worth doing or had it lost its usefulness as cultural utterance, artistic expression, political achievement, or critical material? Why was he Seymour Krim and not Norman Mailer or Mario Puzo or any of his more successful writer friends? In his essay "Making It!" he would observe, somewhat facetiously, that "the only enemy today is failure, failure, failure, and the only true friend is—success?"

To say that Krim was a person of many contradictions is mere understatement. He was a large personality at war, not only with his own being, but with all the ideas in his own head. On the one hand, he dismissed fiction as a kind of has-been activity. A typical observation by Krim regarding fiction was his 1952 essay on Hemingway. In it, he writes: "He is, by our living needs and standards, a true, brilliant, but very limited artist, and I believe that we have gotten all we can from him now." On the other hand, Seymour embraced fiction as the highest literary art form. He wrote that Faulkner's "major contribution" has been his "extreme sophistication in the text itself." Elsewhere, in writing of Jack Kerouac, Krim said: "Jack's stuff often runs like a drunken faucet, but in the flow he gets a love-tone and naturalness that makes most writers blush for their own artificiality." In person, he would seem to be in awe of creative people, especially the real fiction writers among his students. He could become effusive in his enthusiasm about a word or phrase, and madly in love with a paragraph, not to mention expressing his undying love for a complete story that worked well. His standard was of traditions in literature, but he was not in the least offended by anyone kicking out the jams in their writing, going full-on experimental and tearing down the edifice of literary culture that preceded that moment.

In his workshops, he did not present himself as a person wanting to annihilate fiction writing from the planet, but rather as a great nurturer, the one who encouraged young writers, especially the alternative-voiced writer, the writer who was outside the precincts of the establishment. Examples of this generosity of spirit are found throughout his literary essays.

Jerry Jerome (Jerry Roth) described the complexities of Krim's personality beautifully by noting: "He had a good heart wrapped in a bi-polar body."

In the late 1960's, I regularly met up with Jerry at a little gym on 14th Street, playing half-court games of noon-hour basketball, usually with a bunch of older men who were publishers and senior editors, though I never did find out any of their names. When I wasn't playing basketball with Jerry at noon, I went to a tiny boxing gym around 13th Street on the Lower East Side, where I would spar sometimes with highly ranked boxers, sometimes getting the better of them, sometimes getting my ass kicked. When I wasn't doing this, I often met Jerry for drinks at Max's or, now that St. Adrian Company was opened, in that cavernous downtown artist and writer's bar.

Sitting at the bar with Jerry one late afternoon, he recounted his recent run-in with Seymour Krim at the Second Avenue Deli, which sat adjacent to St. Mark's Church. Sometimes he and Krim would grab some deli food and sit in the courtyard of the church, eating and talking shop.

"At other times," Jerry said, "Seymour's eyes would be

rolling in his head like loose furniture on a storm-tossed ship." He paused. "Communication was impossible. He was literally foaming from the mouth."

Despite Krim's often unpredictable nature, his students admired and sometimes even loved him. In terms of that early cohort of writers who had been left after Ishmael Reed moved on, it would seem that the writer Bill Amidon was the link that brought many of them to the Poetry Project's prose workshop. Jerry Jerome told me that it was Bill who had gotten him to attend the workshop. Bill was a rail-thin boozy, cigarette smoking, East Village writer who seemed to know everybody. When I met him, he was probably deep into his thirties, a good number of years older than I was, although there was a youthfulness and energy about him that I admired.

"Amidon was as skinny as a pipe-cleaner armature," Jerry Roth (Jerry Jerome) told me in one of those beer-joint afternoon conversations that we so often engaged in. "But he could drink all night without seeming to get drunk. Sometimes in that period Bill told me there was going to be a writer's group organized at St. Mark's Church, and we went to a preliminary meeting there where Joel Oppenheimer spoke, and talked about the workshops they were setting up and gave out schedules."

The fiction writer John Bart Gerald, already a published book writer at the time of the workshop's inception, came upon Krim's class through Bill Amidon, too. Like Amidon, Gerald lived on 10th Street as rents were cheap.

Once, drinking with him in the Lion's Head, he told me: "My family lived about ten blocks away when I was born and a kid. Some Scot ancestor had a business on the Bowery in eighteen something. After a B.A. (Harvard, *my note*) and reserve training as a medic my unemployment check could pay the rent on 10th Street, so I could write and that's what I was doing there. That was in about '63." Three years later, he found himself involved with the Poetry Project and the fledgling prose workshop through knowing Bill Amidon.

Of the class, Jane Mushabac, another regular at the prose sessions, once told me: "One of the great gifts of the workshop was meeting this incredible and unusual group of people: smart, accomplished, demanding to the point of being frightening, yet surprisingly friendly and warm, many of them with an extraordinary gift for friendship. I think of Clark Whelton and Bill Amidon as well in this regard. My friendship with Janet Chalmers has been very important to me and I've treasured knowing her over the years. Her bold writing appeared years ago in the *Village Voice* (I taught her article on a neighborhood school in my journalism class at Queens College), and now she's writing poetry." Most of the writers at Krim's workshop lived locally, either in the East Village or further west in the more affluent Greenwich Village. A few lived uptown, and maybe even one or two commuted from an outer borough like Brooklyn, Queens, or the Bronx. The ones who lived below 14th Street continued that literary conversation outside the weekly workshop, which usually met on a Monday evening for several hours. Amidon hung out in Max's Kansas City. He drank at the bar, talking to the other writers, and he usually hung out there around the happy hour, from five o'clock in the afternoon onward. This routine would change when St. Adrian Company bar was opened on Broadway near Great Jones Street. Amidon moved in easily, resting his elbows at the bar. So did Jerry Roth. So did a lot of the people who attended the workshops.

Seymour Krim gave everyone permission to use the first person singular, to be themselves in their writing, whether the "self" encompassed radical feminism, Black Power, Jewish angst, Wasp guilt, pornography, or the language of the street. All these voices were heard from within the walls of the Poetry Project's workshops. In other words, Krim gave his students permission to fail, grandly, stunningly, brilliantly. He let everyone rant I, I, I in order to find their voice. Krim's friend Dan Wakefield, fellow New Journalist with Seymour, once made observations that I find apposite to what I am saying here. In writing on this topic of voice, Wakefield said that "the 'I' is something we commonly consider a luxury, reserved for Faulkners, Einsteins, or Eisenhowers who have earned by their professional achievement the right to express their opinion on something." But then Wakefield goes on to quote from Henry David Thoreau: "It is, after all, always the first person that is speaking." In Krim's workshops, he let his students know that it was, after all, always the first person that spoke from their writings, even when they masked it with the third person or some other rhetorical device.

Bill Amidon was an important member of the workshop, not just for his literary contributions. As I have noted, he was the person who brought many of the writers to the early sessions. He exemplified the spirit of experimentation as well as a dedication to finding his own voice. But he also shared a seemingly collective grudge that all the young writers had towards the Establishment, however one defined such an amorphous opposition. For Bill and the others, the clearest form of resistance was to the government and its ever-expanding war in Southeast Asia. But resistance also took the form of cultural allegiances, the downtown literary scene preferred to anything uptown and mainstream. As a result, Amidon was a regular in several downtown saloons, including Max's and St. Adrian's, but also a string of dives on Second Avenue and the even cheaper ones on Avenue B. Perhaps that was another thing that Seymour Krim seemed to pass on to his young writers, that sense of grand, noble failure being a kind of literary badge of honor. As Joel Oppenheimer was drinking himself to death in the Lion's Head in the Village's Sheridan Square, Bill Amidon was matching him, drink for drink, in the dives of the East Village and its vicinity.

There was an impressive range of women's voices in Krim's workshop, perhaps the most varied of all the voices in attendance, ranging from Grace Rooney's Joycean experiments in "Death of the Father" to Rascha Levinson's coolly brilliant, intellectual journey, "Description of a Situation." Janet Chalmers' "Tourist Notes" deftly explored the emotions surrounding a random suicide. Jane Mushabac was yet another one of these woman's voices. Her story "Sunday" is a quiet meditation on sisterhood as one woman strolls Central Park on a crowded Sunday, searching for her sibling, her other. Nothing much happens in the story, and yet by the end of the piece, there is a sense of closure, of finality, of the narrator coming to terms with herself.

Under Grace Paley's tutelage, Sarah Kernochan had been given writers like Isaac Babel and Flannery O'Connor to read. She had a wide range of fiction reading under her belt before coming to the workshop, and so her writing seemed to reflect that literary education. Her prose was moody and full of sly references to the blues, as she also fronted a blues band that sometimes played in a club on Eighth Avenue in the Fifties, just north of Times Square. Although her work did not appear in Krim's workshop anthology *Survival Prose*, she did publish a novel entitled *Dry Hustle* (1977), about the sex trade in Times Square. She also recorded several albums, *House of Pain*, *Beat Around the Bush*, and *Decades of Demos*, as well as penning a string of movie scripts, including *9 ½ Weeks*.

Kernochan's writing and creative output typified the live-for-the-moment attitudes that saturated the East Village, not to mention Seymour Krim's prose workshop, in those days. Her writing was bawdy, even raunchy, energetic, and exceedingly well written.

As this was the late 1960s, the dominant voices were still male, though that was abruptly about to change. Most of these male writers were included in the *Survival Prose* anthology, with a few exceptions. Although Marshall Blonsky did not present his nonfiction works in Krim's workshop, the atmosphere of the class had to have had some influence on his writing. Blonsky's book *American Mythologies* (1992) is a kind of homegrown recasting of the French work *Mythologies* by Roland Barthes. John Bart Gerald had already published a novel while a very young man, and what the workshop did for him was to change his more traditional way of writing prose to a more dedicated approach to experimentation; he would stop publishing commercially, and only publish books that were written and made by him and his partner, Julie Maas, their imprint called Editions Gerald and Maas, away from the political mess of the United States in Canada. Jerry Roth (Jerry Joth/ Jerry Jerome) would go on to write a series of soft-porn novels such as *Lady Dick*, about a female detective, publishing with the legendary Maurice Gerodias at Olympia Press. Bill Amidon published his novel, *Charge…!*, with Bobbs-Merrill, the same company that would publish *Survival Prose* (1971), the fiction anthology that came mostly out of Krim's workshop. But like so many writers of this time and place, Bill Amidon's life would prove to be a short one, abbreviated mostly by Bill's drinking.

Besides the strong feminist and gay voices in Seymour Krim's workshop, traditional male voices were heard in writers like Clark Whelton and John Bart Gerald, though Whelton would move away from fiction entirely and become a New York journalist shortly, and Gerald would become far more experimental in his style and content after his time in the workshop. Marshall Blonsky would represent the purely intellectual pursuits of the writers in the workshop as Shulamith Firestone did the radically feminist ones. David Nemec, a latecomer to the workshops, seemed to represent the emerging voice of the disgruntled soldier as a result of the escalating Vietnam War in his story "Sleep of Soldiers" in *Survival Prose*. Although the voice of Vietnam War soldiers did not play a big part in the prose writing workshop at St. Mark's, nonetheless it was there, if nothing more than a strong undercurrent in the mood of the room. Several of the participants had already served in the military before Vietnam; others would filter in, still trying to work out, not only their voice and register, but the emotional content of their time in combat or, more simply, in the war zones' rear areas, clerk typists who were moving targets for the Vietcong.

Finally, there was that element of the Lower East Side, so essential, its lifeblood, really, the jazz of it, the razzmatazz, its energy and emotion, and that was the burgeoning Black culture as filtered through the hippie scene of the East Village. Everyone I knew, myself included, was influenced by the downtown voices of Black writers, classically from writers like James Baldwin, and more recently from the highly influential LeRoi Jones (Amiri Baraka). The prose workshop began on a high note in this regard, as Ishmael Reed was the first fiction-writing teacher before Seymour Krim. (Reed would go on to an illustrious prose career as one of the great Black comedic voices in 20th century American writing.) The other prose writer before Seymour Krim was Steve Cannon, a brilliant and brilliantly funny person and writer. Yet in the midst of this vibrant alternative culture that the Lower East Side had become, Black culture was only represented by dissonant voices from the Umbra poets, now almost completely disappeared, while Jones/ Baraka had his Black Arts theater scene, first, uptown, and then shortly thereafter in Newark. The Five Spot Café, Slugs, the Old Reliable, and a couple of other jazz venues featured the very best in avant-garde jazz and new Black music, and their audiences included hip, young Black artists, musicians, and even writers, but the Poetry Project at St. Mark's was not reflecting this part of the zeitgeist with anything resembling fidelity.

If I were to offer a general criticism of St. Mark's Poetry Project, it would be that it never included enough Black voices in its networks. (I am speaking about its early days in the mid-1960s.) The writing scene at the Poetry Project seemed almost negligent in its pursuit of such voices. In that sense, the grant remit to attract "(1) alienated youth presently member of the 'subculture of the uncommitted,' and, (2) youth indigenous to a poverty community," had failed miserably in attracting African American writers to the workshops.

Joel Oppenheimer's poetry workshop had nurtured and developed Tom Weatherly's quirky, original voice, culminating in the publication of his *Mau-Mau American Cantos* (1970). But the prose workshop had an almost exclusively white cast to it until the African American writer George Cain showed up one night. Cain was tall, handsome, athletic-looking, edgy from the street, and obviously familiar with the marginal side of urban life, as his prose almost exclusively chronicled the inner workings of uptown drug culture, not the nickel-and-dime marijuana trade of the hippies, but the winner-take-all, loser-take nothing, live-free-or-die mentality of the seasoned junkie, the heroin pusher, the heroin addict, the hookers who linger at the periphery, as well as their pimps. Hearing George Cain read his prose for the first time was something akin to hearing Jimi Hendrix play the guitar. The experiences are not something you soon forget.

There are two writers who come to mind when I recall that time and place that I spent going to the prose workshops offered by Seymour Krim. Both George Cain and Shulamith Firestone sporadically attended the classes, and yet they both had an impact on the workshop, mainly from the energy and intelligence of their writings. Perhaps I mean this observation as being more historical than at that moment. At that moment, George and Shulamith were just two other voices in the group. George was the prose writer par excellence of the crew; Shulamith was the nonfiction writer and thinker, her radical feminist vision really the overriding one of this time and place known as the Sixties decade and the East Village of downtown New York.

When George Cain began to show up at the prose workshop, he read excerpts from *Blueschild Baby* (1970), the novel he would publish shortly. Here was a writer who had poetry in his voice, along with the urgent cadences of a John Lee Hooker blues shout, a Leadbelly folk-song, a raunchy Chicago blues as played by Junior Wells or Little Milton. Cain had it all in one prose style, a gift beyond measure, as they say.

"A sickness comes over me in this twilight state, somewhere between wake and sleep, my nose runs and my body screams for heroin. It is an internal nervous disorder which floods the brain and short circuits senses. I infect the world with it."

If there is poetry in George Cain, it is of the pared-down prose kind, just the facts, no metaphors out of whack, no elongated asides puffed up with the young writer's pleasure at his own cleverness. George came into the workshop a full-blown writer, but also with full-blown demons on both shoulders, and death breathing down his back. He had that Robert Johnson gift of being at the crossroads with the devil, and everything he wrote reflected this personal torment.

"I dump the stuff in the cooker, add water, cook, and tie up. Then draw most of the solution into the dropper. I plunge it into my arm, popping and crackling as it tears through old scar tissue, then the click of a punctured vein and I squeeze the bulb."

There was plenty of street savvy in Krim's workshop, but George Cain seemed to be just a good bit tougher, more worldly, with-it, hip, lyrical, and streetwise than anyone else in the room. He was that disaffected youth that the Poetry Project's sociologists had dreamed about when they made their grant application to the federal government's Department of Health, Education and Welfare. There was a mystery about George, and he promulgated it further by not telling anyone anything more about himself than that he was there, and once he read his story and the class ended, he would be gone again, maybe for another week until they met again, maybe never to be seen again, his name emerging years later. Though his prose appeared to be more influenced by William Burroughs than LeRoi Jones, nonetheless he was authentically portraying a certain kind of Black, urban experience. But what is most remarkable about Cain's writing is how even Seymour Krim's influence is there, as witness this bit of dialogue by Sun, the dealer/pimp uptown where the narrator goes to score. Sun says:

"When I heard you were fucking around, couldn't believe it. Georgie Cain, the intellect, big time basketball star, it was a bitter pill baby."

George Cain would not publish another novel after his first one, *Blueschild Baby*, his life dictated by his drug addiction; he would live to be sixty-six years old, dying in 2010. Although he would not reveal any details of his personal life when he attended Krim's prose workshop at St. Mark's, I would learn more than forty years later, reading his obituary in the *New York Times*, that his real name was George Maurice Hopkins and that he "was born in Manhattan on Oct. 27, 1943, and grew up in the Hell's Kitchen neighborhood. His father, an employee with the Department of Labor, ascended the civil service ladder and reached the position of assistant regional manager, a job that allowed him to move the family to a middle-class neighborhood in Teaneck, N.J., soon after George graduated from high school." I also learned from the obituary that Cain had played college basketball, which I knew, at Iona College, which I didn't know, after a scholarship to a prep school in Manhattan, something he did talk about to people in the workshop. Cain was *sui generis* among Lower East Side writers, and like Shulamith Firestone, very much a loner, going his own way with everything. He was certainly the most gifted of the prose writers who wrote fiction in Seymour Krim's prose workshop at St. Mark's.

Shulamith Firestone's *Dialectic of Sex* (1970) was a much discussed book a few short years after her attendance at the prose-writing workshop. Firestone was twenty-five when her feminist manifesto was published, and it was a transformative work whose influence is still felt today. But like so many others in the workshop, from Seymour Krim to Bill Amidon, Shulamith Firestone's spin out was not from drugs, as it would be for George Cain, but rather her mental illness. She would spend the rest of her life, more or less, living in an East Village tenement, a paranoid hallucination straight out of Allen Ginsberg's *Howl*. Her life typified the failure artist of Krim's prose, and yet in fact she was an incredibly successful writer and thinker, exerting an influence on the late 20th century's ideas like almost no one else out of the East Village in those days.

From the time Firestone arrived in the East Village in the 1960s until her death in 2012, she never really left the Lower East Side. It clearly was her home, however imperfect that concept. Writing about her in the *New York Times*' obituary, Margalit Fox observes that Firestone's "only other book *Airless Spaces* was issued in 1998 by the experimental publisher Semiotext(e). A memoir-in-stories that employs fictional forms to recount real-life events, it describes Ms. Firestone's hospitalization with schizophrenia, which by the 1980s had overtaken her." Though *Airless Spaces* would be misunderstood by many critics, Shulamith Firestone had returned to many of the ideas that were regularly bandied about in Seymour Krim's workshop, the semifictional, first-person narrative, the dedication to experimentalism, the fictionalized self at the center of it. In many ways, she had become the ideal workshop member no matter how much she balked at the chauvinism and male dominance, not just in the workshop but in the world around her.

Much of Firestone's career was extra-literary, having to do with her political beliefs. But as Susan Faludi pointed out in *The New Yorker* after Firestone's death, she was rejected on two fronts in her lifetime—by her biological family and by the very organization she helped to found. Of the former, I heard a great deal, as there was a period during the time she attended Krim's workshop in late 1967 when we hung around together. We had a brief affair that lasted one night, drinking wine after the workshop, several bottles, and then having sex on the hard workshop table, its hardness mollified by my sleeping bag. Shulamith uttered one of the great lines that I still remember, more than fifty years later. "Let's get one thing clear, Stephens," she told me. "I'm fucking you, you aren't fucking me." I was in love with her wild jew-fro hair and her piercing eyes that night, her compactness. We were joined by a mutual hatred of the traditional family, both of our writings out to annihilate that patriarchal structure, hers with her feminist manifesto, mine with my first novel, *Season at Coole*, published two years after her *Dialectic of Sex* came out. We drank wine; we fucked on the hard table. She was fucking me; I was not fucking her. When it was over, she stumbled out of the room and went home.

It was the last I ever saw her, as she soon after that stopped attending the workshop. In reading her later work, *Airless Spaces*, published almost thirty years after *The Dialectic of Sex*, I realize that she had no interest in me. It was Seymour Krim who she was in love with. In her story "Sheldon Krem," she wrote: "I should have married that guy. Or at least had a deep affair with him." When their romance did not pan out, Shulamith wrote that Krim "became less interested in my writing." I now see that I was the beneficiary of that falling out on that night in which we got drunk on several bottles of wine, made love, and then she disappeared from my life. My ego let me believe that it was I who drove her away from the workshop but, no, no, it was Krim, our teacher, who had been too eager or not eager enough.

"I was a buxom Jewess with glasses like his and long frizzy hair," she wrote, "aggressive in some ways but shy."

That night I admired her fierceness, her ferocity, her burning focus, and how anger exuded from her the way I also seethed with determination and damnation.

Shulamith was born in Canada, came from a large Orthodox Jewish family, and grew up in the Midwest, in such places as St. Louis. She studied at the Art Institute in Chicago and Washington University in St. Louis, and came to New York in 1967. She was also one of the founders of several women's organizations, including Redstockings and the New York Radical Feminists. After being rejected as the leader of one of these organizations she founded, she withdrew from public life shortly after *The Dialectic of Sex* was published, having almost nothing to do with the dialogue which ensued. When she died, Firestone was penniless and starving, suffering from schizophrenia. Unlike Seymour Krim, who found himself in a similar circumstance when he was young, but who found his own transformation in a beautiful dance by a young Polish woman in Newark, Shulamith Firestone had no such transformative occurrence. Alone, forgotten, broke, she died at the age sixty-seven in August 2012.

Firestone found the workshops politically unenlightened for her radical nature. She left the workshop months after attending it with some regularity. Almost immediately after she left the writing workshop, she began to emerge in various feminist circles as a key figure in this movement. Historically she is considered one of the founders of second-generation feminism, circa the late 1960s. Then came the publication of her book, *The Dialectic of Sex*, a scathing critique of male/female relationships, from the intimate to the public. It was a book that seethed with her fierce intelligence and her uncompromising political positions. The book was both unique and somehow typical of its time and place. Though *The Dialectic of Sex* did not seem to fit the pattern of writers in Krim's workshop, her only other book (*Airless Spaces*) later in her career, was a book of stories that very much embraced the experimental nature of most of the writers in the Krim prose workshop at the Poetry Project. *Airless Spaces* very much typifies the kind of writing that took place in Seymour Krim's Poetry Project prose workshop. The prose was subjective and interior, a brilliant, broken, terrifying, Cassandra-like voice, shouting to us from the wilderness, both of the time and of her mind. Her later writing was characterized by a semi-fictional "I," in other words, total imaginative writing, the eternal nature of the present tense, the idea of writing occupying the one tense universe, the present tense, the subjective "I," the "I" of Joan Didion, the "I" of George Orwell, and the eye of Seymour Krim, the eye/I of Shulamith Firestone.

If the term *total imaginative writing* seems like a coded message in a men's club, I would disagree. Krim's workshop was not run like Oppenheimer's class, in which the rules of the Wild West were in operation. If anything, Krim's workshop was a clear example of multiculturalism, of men's and women's voices operating simultaneously and equally in concert with one another, if not harmoniously, then certainly together, not in unison, but in a group, counter-pointing each other. Shulamith Firestone cut her literary teeth in our class, however briefly, however discordantly with the others in the room, Krim included. She was not a person who would tolerate being submerged in male-dominated ideas of prosody and the poetics of prose. She was a fierce intellectual presence, not just in the workshops at St. Mark's Church, not just at the Poetry Project, but throughout the newly emerging downtown feminist world, of which she played so important a central part, being one of its most radical and key figures. Shulamith Firestone was not so much typical of the prose writing at the St. Mark's workshop as she was an exemplary voice in the downtown world, encompassing the old radicalism of the immigrant Jews of the historical Lower East Side along with the newer sensibilities of feminism in the East Village. No one had as fierce and intellectually resonant a voice as Shulamith Firestone did in 1967-1968. Unlike the workshop participants, all of whom were writers to a woman or a man, Firestone was both a writer *and* a thinker. Her ideas were as incendiary as gelignite bombs.

If there are differences between the poets and prose writers at St. Mark's, they are superficial ones. I am reminded, once again, of that great Jack Kerouac quote about the rhythm of poetry, and its rush. Kerouac makes no distinction between prose or poetry here, saying, "whether it is a poem in verse-separated lines, or an endless one-line poem called prose." I see the one-line poem called prose as being the key to all the writing in Krim's workshop. But I also see the one-line poem called prose as being a key to Seymour Krim's own writing, his objections to affinities with Jack Kerouac aside. Krim's idea of total imaginative writing is another way of saying the one-line poem called prose that Jack Kerouac wrote about. Total imaginative writing or the one-line poem called prose, this is the method that was promulgated at St. Mark's, both in the poetry and the prose workshops, whether it was Bill Amidon or Bart Gerald, George Cain or Shulamith Firestone.

V.

THE TIME OF THE ASSASSINS

we turn our
backs on each other so often,
we destroy any community of
interest.
—Joel Oppenheimer

V

THE LINK OF THE ASSASSINS

One night I got into a conversation with Sarah after the workshop, and somehow I convinced her to drop out of Sarah Lawrence College and go to San Francisco. "We'll sing in the sunshine," I said. She was game; she was in. Six feet tall, with long straight blonde hair, she had a penchant for velvet bell-bottom pants and jackets, with ruffled white linen blouses, very Londonesque, very British—very rock 'n' roll. Both of us were Irish and influenced by lush writing. But otherwise we were like chalk and cheese, she a child of privilege versus me a Brooklyn street kid, stinking of poverty and, though sometimes charming, full of resentments. Full of conspiracies. Full of plots. Full of shit. She gave me the money to buy two airline tickets to California, and we agreed to meet up at my friend Ron Edson's apartment on Sullivan Street in the South Village, just below Houston Street.

The day came, but I was nowhere to be found.

I had spent all the money on drugs and alcohol, and wound up calling Sarah at her home in Greenwich, Connecticut.

Much to my surprise, she seemed to forgive me for my indiscretions. She even told me that her mother liked my voice when I called and the mother had answered the telephone.

That was in December 1967. By February of the new year, I was in New England, no longer homeless, I was a guest of the MacDowell Colony in Peterborough, New Hampshire. I was twenty-one years old, and turned twenty-two while in residence at the artist and writers' retreat in snow-bound northern New England.

I wore Cuban military fatigues, best suited for the tropics, not really effective in the cold, clear, invigorating air of New Hampshire, so I wore several sweaters and a sweatshirt underneath my Cuban jacket. An older brother had given me the Cuban fatigues after he took a job working in an anti-poverty program of the Johnson Administration, the same benefactors of the Poetry Project. With several layers under the jacket and pants, I managed to survive in the blisteringly cold New England winter. I never discovered how my older brother acquired a set of Cuban military fatigues in an anti-poverty program in White Plains.

I wrote poems in my studio and also the first draft of a novel, which I was not sure where it was going, although a lot of it had to do with my experiences of working on a ship and sailing to the Mediterranean whose cities I would return to every twenty-one days. I thought of Eugene O'Neill, whom I emulated. I thought of Che Guevara, whom the CIA assassinated in South America, and they photographed him, a slab of meat on the embalming table, but he now was a cross between David's Marat and one of Caravaggio's saints. At least that is what I read somewhere or another with regard to that photograph of the revolutionary leader. The US government had intended the photo to be cautionary; instead it had become iconic, the purest revolutionary inspiration. Che had ascended into heaven in very much the same way that Remedios the Beauty ascended into heaven in Gabriel Garcia Marquez's *One Hundred Years of Solitude*, the wind blowing the laundry, then Remedios ascending.

I wrote letters to Sarah when I wasn't working on the book manuscript.

One night at the MacDowell Colony, just before dinner, I put this quote by Fidel Castro on the bulletin board. "The duty of the revolutionary is to make the revolution."

The next morning it had already been taken down.

Immediately several of the older colonists took umbrage with my ways, claiming that I was unduly politicizing their community, bringing the bad energies of New York City into the pristine beauty of New England. They called me many things, a little shit, a smug bastard, a communist, a left-wing lunatic, and a misguided youth.

In the mail I had received a copy of Allen Van Newkirk's broadsheet *Guerrilla* and posted it on the bulletin board. It had that quote about Poetry Is Revolution / Revolution Is Poetry, with photographs of LeRoi Jones/Amiri Baraka's bashed-in skull from the police violently arresting him during the Newark riots a few years before, as well as the poems a judge claimed had caused the riots. Almost immediately the broadsheet was removed, and the director of the colony asked to speak with me, wanting to know if I was happy there. Perhaps I was too young for this intense, singular experience, he suggested. Perhaps I needed to go back to the East Village to mature sufficiently before I came back to MacDowell. I was reminded that I was very fortunate to be the youngest person ever admitted into the writers and artists' colony. I was moments away from turning a very old twenty-two.

"You don't want to become the youngest person ever thrown out of here, do you, Mr. Stephens?" "No, I don't, sir," I said. "I like being here, and I'm grateful to you and your board. But there are two wars going on in America right now, and it's foolish to ignore either one of them." The director was an older waspy-looking man in rimless glasses, with the dour countenance of an undertaker or a Protestant minister from this region. "I'm aware of the war in Vietnam," he said, looking down his nose at me with immense condescension and annoyance. "Remind me of the other one."

"America is at war with its cities," I said.

"Is that so?"

He looked quite amazed at my remark.

"What exactly do you mean, Mr. Stephens?"

I looked at him with great alarm in my face, as if I were going to tell him something that he did not know and perhaps he would not like.

"America is at war with its Black citizens," I said.

"And why should that be any of your business?"

"We are all Americans," I said. "American culture is Black culture. Without Black culture we would be nothing more than imitators of European sensibilities."

The director paused.

"Let me say this, Mr. Stephens, the colony is for all the colonists, not just you. The bulletin board is for everyone, not you alone. If you misbehave," and he said that word in a way as to suggest that I was quite infantile and he was quite superior to my pratfalls, which nonetheless he was no longer going to tolerate: "I shall be forced to withdraw our invitation for you to be here. You will be asked to leave."

"I see," I said, but there was nothing more for me to say because the director, almost like he were a rector of a posh boys' school that was about to expel me for my misconduct, stood and opened the door to his office and gestured with his free hand for me to arise and go, and go now back out to my cottage to write, which I did.

Several of the colonists were forty and fifty years older than I was. The closest colonists in age to me were an abstract painter and an experimental writer, both of them in their early thirties. I often played ping-pong and smoked dope with the writer, Rudy Wurlitzer. His studio was near mine, and sometimes we played basketball games in his studio, using wadded up pages of his manuscript as the ball, the wastebasket the bucket. Rudy had played basketball at Columbia, and I could see he was still good. He was on the verge of having his first novel *Nog* published by Random House, and he was already getting involved in the movie business on the West Coast. He had lent me a copy of the *Paris Review* in which one of the chapters from the novel appeared, and when he wasn't working on revising his novel, we talked in the main house, as we seemed to know a lot of people in common from places like Max's Kansas City. He also knew Robert Creeley and Max Finstein (he of the Max's Kansas City name) from his times in New Mexico. Though from New York City, Rudy seemed oriented towards the West, kind of like the playwright Sam Shepard, who later became a good friend of his. Rudy was tall and balding, and he reminded me of the painter Jackson Pollock, though his temperament was more laid back than the mad-genius artist and drinker of Abstract Expressionism.

Rudy had gone off to Hollywood for a week, and planned to return that evening. He would be at the nearby Keene Airport, and he needed someone to pick him up. Ken volunteered to get him before Rudy left for Hollywood. The two of them regularly played ping-pong in the evening, and I would play the winner. Invariably Rudy won. Ken asked if anyone would accompany him because he was not entirely sure of the route to the airport. No one stepped up. Finally I agreed to go. I went upstairs and got my Cuban fatigue jacket and my knitted cap and gloves, put on my boots, and met Ken out by his car. We drove off into the night, searching for the airport. But it was snowing, the visibility not good, and we got lost. Ken pulled into a gas station to ask for directions, and unbeknownst to us, a state trooper observed us, decided we were suspicious and followed us to the airport.

The airport was a tiny operation, a wind sock, a hangar or two, the runway, and the surrounding airstrip. The plane landed, and Rudy emerged down the steps carrying a suitcase and a shoulder bag. He schlepped the bags towards Ken's car, and as he was putting them into the trunk, lights began to flash, sirens went off, a policeman stood facing us, his gun drawn and pointed towards us. We stood frozen in the night, as the cop approached us, backlit by his headlights on high beams. He was a big cop, mean and no-nonsense. (That is how I read the situation, in any event.) He made it known right away that he didn't like outsiders in his state and he didn't like hippies. He especially did not like hippies. While Rudy's hair was short, both Ken and I had long hair and beards. The cop got us to put our hands on the cold top of the car, to spread eagle, while he searched for weapons or, as he said, contraband.

The cop finished his body search and found no weapons. We thought that would be the end of it. Now he made Ken open the trunk of his car, and the trooper searched there. His flashlight probed the interior of the car. Lord knows what he was looking for. But then I guess he found what he wanted. He asked Rudy to open his suitcase, which Rudy did, and the trooper rifled through it until he found some marijuana, pills, opiates, whatever. We were cuffed and put in the back of his car and taken to the county jail where we were finger-printed and booked. I was charged with being an accessory to a crime, as was

Ken, and Rudy got the book thrown at him for possession of marijuana and other illegal substances.

We were deemed dangerous, so each one of us was put into his own cell, though the cells were next to each other, so we were able to talk back and forth. When I was able to make a telephone call, I called Ron Edson and asked him to spread the word. I might need help. I am not sure how long we actually spent there in the Keene county jail. But I know it felt like an eternity. Now I was bereft of poetry or prose, my typewriter, my ream of foolscap, my pens and notebooks, all gone. What I had was a book of poems in one pocket of my jacket that somehow the state trooper forgot to confiscate. And I had a pen.

All my other possessions had been removed from me, including my shoes and my belt. The floor in the jail was cold, the blankets on the bed were thin, the mattress was lumpy, the toilet smelt of other men's urine, and I was miserable.

The one book that I had in jail was by John Ashbery. It was called *Rivers and Mountains*. Scott Cohen, from Joel Oppenheimer's poetry writing workshop at St. Mark's, had recommended that I read it. He particularly liked a long, lyrical poem called "The Skaters," which Scott deemed a masterpiece. "It is full of ideas from Wittgenstein's philosophy," he said, and so while I was at MacDowell and when I finished writing for the day, I would read this book, particularly that poem, trying to fathom what Scott Cohen and Andrei Codrescu, and so many others of my friends, found so interesting about Ashbery's poetry. I was still at a loss to determine what it was they liked so much about his work, although I had to admit that I now had come across a handful of his poems that I thought remarkable. With *Rivers and Mountains*, I still struggled. But, in that sense, it was a good book to have on hand in a New Hampshire jail. I had lots of time; the place was quiet and we were left undisturbed as, behind the scenes, Rudy's family and their lawyers worked to get us free. So I read John Ashbery when I was not shouting back and forth to Rudy and Ken in the other cells at the county jail in Keene. I wrote things in the margins of the book, as I had no other paper, but somehow managed to keep a pen on me. I attempted to read "The Skaters." I read: "On the secret map the assassins / Cloistered…"

Ezra Pound once said that a writer could not have too many experiences. Being in jail in New Hampshire was one too many experinces, though. It was an unnecessary experience, and yet I decided to make the most of my incarceration. I thought about the book I had been writing and how I might continue it and how I might revise it. I was already into the second draft. I also became paranoid. When I was let out of my cell for an hour or two, able to pace in the walkway in front of the cells, I became silent around Rudy and Ken. I thought maybe they were conspiring to pin this "crime" on me, the young guy wearing the Cuban military fatigues. Rudy tried to assure me that it was all his fault; he had been careless about how he transported his possessions. He told me that his family was working with a lawyer to get bail for the three of us. Somehow he convinced me not to worry. The day arrived when our bail was posted and we were released, scheduled to appear in court in Keene in the near future. We drove back to the MacDowell Colony in Ken's car. But almost as soon as we arrived, we each were told that our fellowships had been cancelled. We had to vacate the property once we packed up our possessions from the writing and painting cottages and from our rooms in the main house. I don't know where Ken planned to go, but Rudy told me that I could catch a ride with him to New York City, where he was going. He had a sports car, a Triumph, and we drove down through New England into New York state, and then into the city. Rudy dropped me off in Sheridan Square, where I stood like a prodigal son. I walked across the street towards the Lion's Head on Christopher Street, figuring I might know someone in there. As soon as I crossed Seventh Avenue South and stood in front of the *Village Voice*'s main office, I saw Sarah who was now working at the newspaper, right next to the bar. It was the first time I had seen her since I disappeared with her money for the plane tickets to San Francisco. She let me know right away that there were no hard feelings, so I explained to her what had just happened. We had been in touch with each other via the mails while I was working on the book at the MacDowell Colony. But communications had gone silent after being arrested.

We left it that I would be in touch with her after she got out of work around five that evening. I said goodbye and went into the Lion's Head to have a word with Joel.

"Machine Gun," Oppenheimer shouted, as I came down the couple of steps into the dark bar. "What brings you in?"

After a few more drinks, I wandered off to a pawn shop on 14th Street where I sold my binoculars that some people at the Poetry Project had given me before going off to MacDowell. I thought of pawning my typewriter but that was too self-effacing, and I had not yet become a total doormat towards myself. That evening I returned to the *Voice* office in that pie-shaped building at the corner of Seventh Avenue and Christopher Street on Sheridan Square. Sarah and I walked to the East Village through the romance of Washington Square, and the elegant squalor of the Lower East Side. We made love immediately, and then I slept. The apartment belonged to a writer friend of Grace Paley's, and he was an essayist and political commentator, so the apartment was filled with books, many of which I read while Sarah was at work. This arrangement lasted only a short time, until the writer unexpectedly returned from his assignment abroad, and we had to find another place to live. Sarah went looking and came up with a studio apartment on St. Marks Place (remember: no apostrophe) near Avenue A. Still having to go back to New Hampshire to face a drug trial, I began to rewrite my book in that tiny apartment at the center of the zeitgeist.

It was from the vantage point of St. Marks Place that I learned about the death of Martin Luther King in Memphis on April 4, 1968. The aftermath of his assassination was the opposite of all his ideas on nonviolence, though. As the historian Peniel E. Joseph notes: "The tally of destruction in the wake of King's death was overwhelming—125 cities in twenty-nine states experienced racial unrest, and estimated $45 million in property damage was reported. The human cost included thirty-nine dead and three thousand five hundred injured." As was true with other 1960s riots, cities bore the brunt of the violence and destruction, and New York had its share of rioting. I remember meeting Sarah at the *Voice* and walking back to her new studio flat. As I walked across Cooper Square, there was an eerie calm, as if being in the eye of a storm, and by the time we got back to the studio apartment, the streets were awash in insurrectionary sentiments. Much of the Black response was rhetorical, but out on the street, one moved cautiously, especially as I was walking beside a wrathelike, six-feet tall blonde in velvet bellbottoms.

At the time of King's assassination, he had been vilified by the Black Power leaders, from Eldridge Cleaver to Stokely Carmichael. King's brand of revolt was deemed candy-assed, although, in 1968, I still believed that he had the best way possible to improve so many social injustices in America, from race relations to the war in Vietnam. In other words, I probably mourned the death of Martin Luther King more than any other 1960s political leader, including the two Kennedys and Malcolm X. (Bobby Kennedy would be killed a few months after King's death.) I loved the rhetorical power of Martin Luther King's speech, but I also liked his philosophical underpinnings that went back to Gandhi and, in a more American way, back to Henry David Thoreau. I saw Dr. King as a living, breathing link with the radical ideas of Thoreau. So while a lot of my neighbors used the occasion of King's assassination as the reason to riot, I was certainly made more reflective by the assassination, going further inward, as I holed up in the tiny studio apartment and rewrote my book as Sarah went off to work each morning at the *Village Voice* in Sheridan Square. The time would come when I had to return to work at the bookshop. But for the moment, I was simply a writer and nothing else. I had several hundred pages of a manuscript, which I was determined to complete before I got back into the flow of work, earning a living, being responsible, paying rent, buying food, having a relationship with another human being. Was it love? Was it merely transactional, two random humans meeting at a prose workshop a few months earlier? I definitely liked Sarah. A lot. Her humor was dry and raunchy, bawdy and over-the-top. She was a singer besides being a writer, and she was way out and willing to go further out. She was up for anything, in a certain sense, especially if it involved music or words. I think that was our connection, too; we were both in love with words. Both of us were hungry to know everything, to read everything, to be alive in this moment, even if it was a time of assassins.

Malcolm X had been assassinated in Harlem in February 21, 1965. JFK faced his own assassination from the backseat of a Lincoln convertible on November 23, 1963 in Dallas. Now it was Martin Luther King's turn to be gunned down by assassins. Two months later it would be Robert Kennedy's turn in the meat-grinder, in the gimlet eye of the assassin, staring into the scope's lens. At night, I held Sarah in my arms, fearful but putting on a brave face, as I suspect she was doing too. We were living in an interesting time.

After being arrested and released on bail, I was once again called up with a draft notice, this time needing to appear at Whitehall Street downtown. Despite being out of shape and drinking too much and smoking dope, I passed the physical. It was the year of the Tet Offensive in which the Viet Cong and North Vietnam had reversed a lot of American gains. If you were still breathing, the Draft Board was going to pass you, and they did. Even with my objections about my psychological state, my moral repulsion for the Vietnam War, and my repugnance for the military for destroying my oldest brother's very good mind, it was to no avail. I was told to report for induction, almost immediately. Apparently I had been put on the fast-track to Vietnam. Within a few days, I bid goodbye to Sarah and went off to Fort Dix in southern

New Jersey. I was given a crew cut, my long curls of hair falling to the ground like black snow. But after one day I was called out of the line by the drill sergeant who wanted to speak to me in his office. Ever since my arrival this man had made my life hell, telling me every chance he got that I was going to be sent to Vietnam where I would honorably give my worthless life for God and country. He had seen me the day before with my long hair and beard, and now I was shorn of everything, a bald assassin.

"You didn't tell me you were a drug addict, Stephens," the sergeant began his tirade.

"Would that have gotten me excluded?" I asked.

"Shut up, shit-for-brains!" he shouted in my face, spitting the words, so that the spray covered my mouth and nose and eyes. "You will talk when I say you will talk, maggot. This is not a conversation. This is not a dialogue, maggot."

I kept my silence. He resumed his tirade.

"You did not tell me you were a drug addict, Stephens. I have an order here telling me that you are under indictment in New Hampshire for being an accessory to a drug crime. Son, you need to take care of this business before I can send your ass to Vietnam to die for God and Country. You will gather your measly shit from your foot locker and return to the scene of your crime, whereby you shall be judged accordingly. If it turns out that you are guilty, then you will serve your time, unless, of course, the judge offers you an option back to Fort Dix and the military, whereby I will shape your sorry ass into a fighting machine for America. If you are found innocent of this crime, which I highly doubt, having seen the condition of your life when you appeared before me yesterday, we will also take your sorry ass back into the ranks of the military, where we will shape that sorry ass into a Man. You are nothing but a pansy right now. The sight of you hurts my eyes."

"Sir?" I asked.

But he would have none of my lip.

"Dismissed!"

I went back to the barracks where I stuffed my few belongings into a duffle bag and walked out the door and off the base and caught a long bus ride back to New York, where I met up with Sarah once again in Sheridan Square. We went into the Lion's Head for a beer. Tom Weatherly came off his job in the kitchen and sat down with us. Joel Oppenheimer came from the bar, Al Koblin the owner sat down with us for a little while. Several other friends, like Ron and Nicki, all wanted to know how come my head was shaved. When I told them, no one believed me. They thought I was telling another one of my stories.

"The Army is hard up right now," Ron said, "because of the Tet Offensive a few months ago, but they ain't so hard up that they would take you into their ranks, Michael."

"True, true," I said, "so maybe I joined Hare Krishna."

Ross Feld asked me to show him the complete manuscript when I had it ready. Now that I was back from my brief jaunt in the military but still not yet being called back to New Hampshire for the trial, I had time to devote to the completion of the manuscript, which is what I did. But in the evenings, I partied with different people or, sometimes, I went along with Sarah to one of her gigs. It was at one of these uptown gigs that I met and became friendly with Arthur Brown, a British rocker who at the time was reprising Screamin' Jay Hawkins' hit, "I Put a Spell on You," Arthur being the first incarnation of the Goths, light years ahead of their arrival in Camden and elsewhere in London and the world. He wore a dark cape and spooky clothing and make-up, making him look like a vampire. I invited him to a reading I was about to do the next evening. I was giving my first Wednesday night reading at St. Mark's Church, with Ron Edson, Jerry Greenberg, Tom Weatherly, and myself. Joel Oppenheimer had selected us from the writing workshop, and then had Anne Waldman set up the particulars of the reading. Arthur Brown came down to the event, wearing his vampire outfit, probably the weirdest guy in the room, no easy feat, especially given how everyone else was pretty strange too. He loved poetry, especially this kind of performance-based poetry that St. Mark's had duly become famous for.

When the reading ended, Ted Berrigan came up to me and shook my hand. I had read from the manuscript that I had been working on at MacDowell and now St. Marks Place. The prose section I read made some passing reference to Sadakichi Hartman living in a teepee in Hollywood. That was the part that Ted Berrigan liked so much.

"I only wish that Frank were still alive," he said. "He would have loved what you read tonight."

Ted wanted to come hang out with us, but I didn't know where the others were going, and I sensed that Jerry Greenberg did not want him coming along. Jerry had created this animus between us and them, the New York School poets, and he was not about to have a pow-wow with their sachem, Ted Berrigan. They disappeared out of the church and around the corner to one of the tiny bars on Second Avenue. I thanked Ted for the praise and said that we'd have drinks another night; I had to catch up with Arthur Brown, Sarah, and the other poets and their friends. "Another time," he said, and went out the door ahead of me. I went up Second Avenue to look for everyone. Although I did not know it at the time, it would be the only time I ever talked directly with Ted Berrigan, other than saying hello to one another on Second Avenue. But it felt good to be part of this downtown scene at the church, and I was glad for his attention. Outside of Joel Oppenheimer, who did not come to the reading, Ted Berrigan was the great mentor and teacher to the young poets at the Poetry Project, and since Frank O'Hara was the one New York School poet whom I read regularly—I should say religiously, as I did it almost every day—it was also good to know that one of his friends, Ted Berrigan, thought so highly of the reading that he said that Frank would have liked what I had read. As I drunkenly walked up Second Avenue, I thought to myself, I have never actually collapsed, thinking of that poem of his about Lana Turner, although I have drunk too much and smoked too much, and been disgracefully intoxicated, as I was then. But I had never actually collapsed, I thought, although I had, nearly at this spot, several years earlier, coming back from an all-night party in Harlem. That morning I had collapsed in front of St. Mark's Church, and I wasn't even Lana Turner. Fortunately, a cabbie saw me fall, put me in his taxi, and rushed me to nearby Beth Israel, where an emergency room doctor saved my life. A few hours later, I walked out of there, back to 10th Street. But that was already a few years ago. This night I did not collapse, I caught up to my friends, and we drank until all hours of the morning.

One Sunday in May, I met Ross Feld at an East Side park where people from Max's Kansas City played softball, a team comprising artists like Dan Christensen, Frosty Myers, and Peter Reginato, as well as the poet Joe Early and the Black Mountain College prose writer and collagist Fielding Dawson. I knew from my friendship with Joel Oppenheimer that everyone at Max's took these softball games seriously, so there was a combination of artistic frivolity and the dead serious on the sidelines and on the field (not of grass but concrete). My manuscript was in a hard 9" x 12" cardboard box that I had purchased in an office supply store downtown. I had entitled the book Up Against the Wall, Motherfucker, in homage to LeRoi Jones (Amiri Baraka), and the novel was ostensibly based on my experiences working on American ships in 1965, what seemed like a millennium past but was only three years ago.

Ross assured me that he would take good care of the manuscript, that he would read it immediately, and get back to me. If he thought the writing worthwhile, he would pass it along to Gilbert Sorrentino, the editor for whom Ross was an assistant. Gil was a well-known downtown poet, and I had several of his books that I cherished. I didn't tell this to Ross, but being published by Grove Press was my dream ever since I had read Samuel Beckett's trilogy of novels when I was fifteen. My friend put the box into a book bag he had and then put the book bag into a very formal looking briefcase and then went back to playing in the softball game. I said hello to a few people I knew, then went on my way.

A few weeks went by.

The telephone kept ringing and ringing, and when Sarah came out of the shower, she picked it up and handed it to me. Hello, I mumbled into the receiver. It was Gil Sorrentino, and he asked if I was Mike Stephens, as he would always call me. Then he asked me: "Is this a bad time, Mike?"

"Can you call me back, Gil."

"When?"

"In a little while," I said.

I hung up and went back to bed. Sarah asked me who had called. I told her. Wasn't he the editor who had my book at Grove Press? He was, I said. Well, don't you think you ought to get out of bed, drink some coffee, and be ready for his call. Why? I asked. He might want to publish your novel, she said. That hadn't occurred to me until she said that, so I got out of bed, brushed my teeth, gargled the stale taste away, drank some coffee, smoked a few cigarettes, and waited for Gil Sorrentino's call back, which he did shortly. He explained that he would like to sign up the book, but things were not so simple at Grove Press. He needed to get Barney Rosset's approval.

"Pinning Barney down is not the easiest thing in the world, Mike, he's as squiggly as a snake. But I'll do my best to get him to come aboard."

"How long do you think it might take?" I asked.

"Don't know," Gil said. "A month or two, six months, a year, two years, he's totally unpredictable. Sometimes he lets the contracts back up for a year or two at a time. Then he signs up everything at once. I'll stay on top of it for you. We have two strong recommendations from me and from Ross Feld, so we'll see how it goes from there. Let's stay in touch."

When I hung up the telephone, Sarah asked what had happened.

"Grove wants to do the novel," I said.

"You need to get an agent," she said.

Sarah always made a lot of sense, and this was no exception. Her advice came at the right moment, and I began to ask around, starting with Seymour Krim, who said he would get back to me. My girlfriend got dressed and went off to work at *The Village Voice*. I wrote some, then made more calls, looking for that elusive bird of paradise known as the literary agent.

It was around this time that Sarah told me that her family, meaning her mother and father, wanted to help my book along, and so offered to let me stay at the family's "cottage" on Martha's Vineyard. "Cottage" is a relative term specific to a place like the Vineyard. I stayed in this big-ass houe on the water, the former summer home of her grandfather. Years later, I would discover that a part of my mother's own family were some of the original settlers on the Vineyard, with names like Doggett and Eddy and Hatch, Cape Cod and Martha's Vineyard names still around today. In 1968, I was this oddball visitor to the cottage. A caretaker and a cook visited me when I arrived. I reminded myself not to get too grandiose, though, as I was only there for a week or two, and then back to New York City to find out if Sarah still planned to hang around with me or not.

During my absence, Sarah found a larger apartment in the Village, a lovely railroad flat on West 10th Street near

Hudson, and moved in. When I got back from the respite on the Vineyard, I joined her in the West Village, showing up at her door with a much fatter manuscript.

Several friends were passing through the city, and they asked to sleep on the couch or floor, so besides the two of us in our new digs, Wayne Oakes showed up from Cortland, New York or wherever he had been journeying or maybe just journaling, and he brought Ardison Phillips along with him. Ardison was a sculptor, Clark's brother, Clark being the person in Syracuse, years earlier, who tried to teach me the lessons of political nonviolence as opposed to personal nonviolence. His analogy was the picket line: if approached by some angry counter-protestor, don't engage them in fisticuffs at the demonstration. Tell them to meet you around the corner, away from the demonstration, and there beat the crap out of them or not. "Muhammad Ali," Clark said. "He's a perfect example. He's antiwar, and yet he earns his living by beating the shit out of people in the boxing ring." I liked the way Clark thought. But I hadn't seen him in years, as he had moved to Canada, not because of the draft—after all, he was a good ten years older than Wayne and me—but to get away from what the United States had become, a country of corporate greed, lacking all ideals. Clark had given up on America entirely and had moved to New Brunswick, Canada. I had met Ardison a few times in Syracuse at his brother Clark's house, and we always got on well. He was several years older than we were, but we all liked to drink and sit around talking and, in Ardison's case, eating. Ardison was full of ideas about everything. While living in Buffalo, New York, he had organized a show at an abandoned supermarket and called it A & P art, showing the paintings and sculptures where the produce and canned goods used to be. He was also into happenings and other theatrical events of the art world. He was a very with-it kind of guy.

I can't remember how long Wayne and Ardison stayed in Sarah's new apartment, but one day she came home from work to find us all sitting around drinking and talking and smoking cigarettes, and she decided that everyone had to go. Everyone packed up and got ready to depart.

"You can stay," she whispered to me, "we're going out, remember?"

"Oh, yeah," I said.

Tall, beautiful, well educated, bookish, even erudite, wickedly and darkly humorous: what was there not to like about Sarah?

After Wayne and Ardison left, I got back to rewriting my book for Grove Press, in the event that they were going to publish it. It was a railroad apartment, and I was given the room next to the kitchen as an office, and the room after that was the bedroom, and it ended in the parlor or living room. I was relieved being in the West Village, away from the temptations of the East Village in the form of people, places, and things, particularly as I had to go back to New Hampshire for the drug trial. I didn't want to be getting myself into any other trouble similar to the Keene, New Hampshire trouble. Every couple of months I had to fly to New Hampshire with Rudy and Ken for another hearing. This would go on for some time. The good thing, though, was that as long as there was an ongoing trial, I still did not have to report back to Fort Dix and the US Army, although I had not heard a word from them since I was sent back to New York for my trial. I was too self-absorbed in those days to realize how kind and generous Sarah was, letting me live there, rent free, with meals thrown in, and with my own office to write in, and as long as I was writing, she seemed okay with me being there and not working at some paying job, although eventually I would need to return to the Eighth Street Bookshop for the six to midnight shift. Yes, I certainly see her kindness and generosity now. But in those days back in the 1960s, I saw everything as my just desserts; everything was owed me, so I took it. I wish I had been kinder and more generous of spirit, looking back on it, but writing is a kind of self-absorption, an indulgence, and I was no different than other writers in searching out a room of one's own. But the room of my own also happened to be in Sarah's apartment. Where was her room of one's own?

Underneath all the good fortune, I still had the trial in New Hampshire to deal with. One day towards the end of the 1960s, I stepped out of the New Hampshire courthouse in a blazing glory of sunshine and spring-like weather, a free man. Technically, I made the decision not to report back to Fort Dix. But the whole thing had been left so vague and uncertain, I decided that I would go back when they contacted me, and not a moment before that. I never heard from New Hampshire, the draft board, or the US Army again. In the autumn of 1968, Sarah and I boarded the Twentieth Century Limited train for Chicago, post convention, a paranoid city of checker-hatted police. Luckily we were not there long, alighting from one train to board the Santa Fe Chief, and to race off in the night southward towards Texas, and then the long slog across the Southwest, up through Needles, California, and eventually de-train in San Francisco, where we were the several-month-long guests of Sujenna, Jerry Greenberg's old girlfriend from East 9th Street, whose other house guest was the editor and writer Charlie Perry, newly working for *Rolling Stone*, an enterprise that Jerry Greenberg had also worked for until his heroin habit reached skyward, and he was eased out of the magazine. Who would not want to be living at Turk and Divisadero near Haight-Ashbury in 1968?

Sujenna, like Janice Joplin, was from Texas. She was ostensibly a school teacher. But she was also many other things. She was, for instance, a champion poker player, a goddess of the nightly mystery novel (just like Jerry Greenberg, her ex-beau); she was also a former stripper in North Beach known as Paxie Peace (with Altamaston stickers for pasties over her nipples, a nonviolent, antiwar stripper, mind you), and a great cook. When I told this story to Charlie Perry many years later, he laughed, and said that Sujenna was putting me on, that she had never been a stripper named Paxie Peace.

Charlie had many hats, literally and figuratively. He was an editor and writer at *Rolling Stone*, he was a genuine California foodie, he was a banjo player, among other instruments, and he spoke and was still learning many different languages. His penchant for languages reminded me of James Joyce, only when I told that to Charlie, he reminded me that James Joyce never could learn Irish, whereas Charlie could. It was while wearing his hat of a foodie that on Thanksgiving day, Charlie discussed making a turkey dinner for all of us. I accompanied Charlie in his beat-up car around San Francisco, looking for a turkey here, cranberry sauce there, stuffing and vegetables elsewhere, so that by the end of the morning, we had visited a Lebanese butcher, a Turkish greengrocer, and a Mexican market. Back at Sujenna's, Charlie made what he called a Virgil Thomson turkey, one that is so blackened by the end of it, it looks inedible, but then proves, underneath the arsonist's bird, to be one of the most juicy turkeys ever cooked.

Like Joel Oppenheimer, Charlie called me Machine Gun, and thus he made a toast to Sarah and Machine Gun, may their visit to San Francisco be a prosperous and enjoyable one. Just then the doorbell rang, and Jerry Greenberg tripped in, high out of his mind, an automatic weapon tucked in his trouser waist. I don't know how she did it, but Sujenna, who had a long history of such behavior with him, got Jerry back towards the door, and then beyond it, whereupon she locked it. The bell rang for a while longer, then he gave up and went away. A few days later, Sarah and I caught a ride with the poet Lewis McAdams down the coast towards Los Angeles, and a few weeks with Ardison Phillips in his downtown artist's loft in Los Angeles. He more than made up for living at Sarah's back in New York by feeding us nightly gourmet meals that he seemed to dream up on the spot. He knew everyone; he even cooked for most of them. He was a human dynamo, involved in an art expo in Osaka, Japan, working with legends like Robert Rauschenberg and Buckminster Fuller. He would yack away about art and technology, and years later I finally understand what he was saying, and why. Shortly after Sarah and I went back to San Francisco, Ardison opened up the Studio Grill restaurant, for a long time, the place where foodies went when they were hungry, and it being West Hollywood, where other people wanted to be seen.

One night that winter I met Hubert Selby, Jr. in Barney's Beanery; Selby was the author of *Last Exit to Brooklyn*. His childhood friend Gilbert Sorrentino had made the introductions via the mails, so Cubby, as his friends called him, knew a little about me from Gil, who was not only his friend but also his literary mentor. Barney's was a dive in West Hollywood made famous by a Robert Keinholz installation that replicated the bar in an art gallery. Music and canned noise was piped into the installation, and instead of human faces the clientele had clock-faces. The real Barney's was a dimly lit bar catering to a West Hollywood crowd, and it was located just off of Santa Monica Boulevard on Holloway, near North Olive. Cubby lived near Barney's, which is why he chose it as a place to meet. But once it filled up and got incredibly noisy, we adjourned to his house nearby.

Selby had one lung because of having tuberculosis in his teens. He was also diabetic, and had just come off a long heroin addiction. Alcohol had become his best friend, so we sat at his kitchen table, drinking away as if there were no tomorrow. We talked deep into the night, in fact, into tomorrow and tomorrow and tomorrow, until his wife Suzanne intervened and scolded her husband and sent me home. The next time I visited, Sarah and I came with Ardison, and he and Cubby would become friends from that time onward. Mostly Selby and I talked about books, Isaac Babel and Herman Melville, authors that Sarah knew better than I did. He also talked about Beethoven, whom he said had exerted an influence upon his writing. That surprised me. He told us about working on ships when he was fifteen years old, and how by eighteen, he was in a German hospital with TB, his lungs diseased and compromised and his prognosis to survive somewhat grim. Doctors told him he had a few months to live. Back in Brooklyn, he took streptomycin to treat the

TB. It kept him alive, but it also impaired his vision and his hearing.

"I went wacky," he said, sounding most Brooklyn. I understood exactly what he meant, being another pure product of that borough.

He told the three of us about his lifelong relationship with Gil Sorrentino, about his novel *Last Exit to Brooklyn* being published. He was out on bail, and so was I. It was another bond we had. A few months after meeting him, Cubby would get sober. But those evenings when I visited him, we drank all night long. He told me about detoxing off of heroin in an LA prison system, and how being an addict was a felony in those days. The brutality of his description of detoxing in prison were chronicled in his incredible novel *The Room*, which he had begun to write already.

Back in San Francisco, I got back into my routine of going to music venues and out of the way restaurants with Charlie Perry. Our mission was to eat as much as we could and then we'd give Charlie any kinds of feedback we wished. He kept elaborate notes on all these adventures, and then paid for everyone by putting it down as business expenses. Thus I ate great Mexican food in the Mission, California fusion cuisine long before such a food existed for everyone else, and even French food occasionally. Charlie took my poems to *Rolling Stone*, and managed to get a few published. I remember one poem I wrote about Joni Mitchell and Bonnard the painter. Then, one day, as a lark, I wrote a so-called journalistic piece about the IRA (then all but dead) supplying guns to the Black Panthers. Sujenna and Charlie had put me up to it, egging me on. I sent it off to the *Village Voice,* and the next thing I knew it had been accepted and published back in New York. Shortly after that, I was visited by the FBI. They came into Sujenna's apartment on Turk Street, wanting to speak to me about the article. How did I come upon this information? I was twenty-two years old, and unsure of what they were entitled to know. I didn't realize that I should have had a lawyer present. I told them that it was a send up, but they did not understand the concept.

"Fiction," I said.

"Where did you meet these people?"

"I never met anyone," I said. "I made it up. There is no IRA element in San Francisco."

The FBI guys wore nondescript dark suits, white shirts, and black ties. They looked more like Mormons than FBI agents. They were only a little older than I was. Probably they had gone to Catholic colleges, then did tours of duty in Vietnam. They seemed as bored by the questioning as I was, and soon left when they could see that they weren't getting anywhere with me. The next thing I knew I was in an Irish neighborhood in the city, Charlie Perry along with me. Some fellow wanted to talk to me, and we entered this corny, sentimental gift shop, a roomful of thick white Irish sweaters from Aran Islands, shamrock coasters, records by the Clancy Brothers, Irish flags, etc. The proprietor locked the shop door and came back to Charlie and me in the center of his store. He had a sacerdotal quality, at first, but the moment the door was locked, he appeared a bit more ferocious. He waggled his meaty right index finger a few inches from my nose, never a good thing to do. Soon enough, he let me know that he was the face of the IRA in San Francisco, and they were not pleased with what I had written about them. How did I know they were supplying munitions to the Black Panthers? he asked me. As with the FBI, I said, "I made it up, it's pure fiction." But it was not pure fiction, it was more science fiction, as I had read the zeitgeist and revealed its hand. Indeed there was a connection with the Panthers and the IRA, according to the FBI and this man in the gift shop, who decided to give me as little information as possible once he determined that I didn't really know a thing about their operations.

The FBI guys were scary, but the IRA guy was much scarier, poking his finger at me, threatening to snuff me out if I stuck my nose in their business again. We left the shop a bit shaken but Charlie knew me and I was not capable of being intimidated by anyone in those days. I was stubborn and determined, and if pushed, I shoved back.

"Fuck him," I said, as we walked to Charlie Perry's car. "Fuck those IRA guys and fuck the FBI."

My next visit came from the Black Panthers. A young fellow approached me in the neighborhood of Turk and Divisadero. It was across the street from the local soul bar, and I was approached on the street by this young fellow who wanted to set up a meeting with me in that bar. The bar at the corner was out of the way and off the beaten path for the hippies and other Haight-Ashbury types. Mostly local Black neighbors drank there. It was dimly lit, just a long bar, and sometimes there was live music. I had been in it a few times because the bluesy live music was often good. But it was plain to me that this was not a good place to hang out. When there was no live music, the juke box was loud, the lights were low, and there was always a stool for a sad-sack man down on his luck or betrayed in love or business, full of pity for himself more than full of the blues.

It was an hour of the day in which not many people frequented the bar. It was the afternoon in San Francisco, and most people had not yet gotten out of work. There was a happy hour in the bar, but that was still a half-hour away when the workers got out for the day. Other than ourselves, there was only one other person at the bar, an old man who was talking to his dog. You could see the neon cocktail glass outside the bar flickering on and off, as if there were an electrical short in the sign, though I suspect that was the way it was always supposed to operate. Inside the bar, it had a darkness fringed by red neon lights, a mirror behind the bar, and at the far end a small stage where the musical acts performed. I ordered a beer, but my young Panther friend declined any alcohol. He told me that he was clean and sober. I toasted him with my beer bottle.

"Bottoms up," I said, and drank.

The young man was not high up in the Panthers. He told me that he was sent to speak to me as a messenger from that group. I think he was maybe a local guy, and he was about my age. We were about the same height and weighed about the same, and both of us had goatees, and wore black leather jackets and had berets. It was just the way I dressed in those days, and I admired the Black Panthers, their style and content. I had read Eldridge Cleaver's *Soul on Ice* several times, and I also had read many articles about Huey Newton, the charismatic leader of the Black Panthers. In order to be a Black Panther, you had to be willing to read for two hours every day. That detail is what most impressed me about them. I liked that detail enormously. Yet I was more a Digger than anything else, that anarchist ball of an organization founded by Emmet Grogan, a Brooklyn native who had migrated to San Francisco some years earlier. The Diggers were political jokers, economic stand-ups, anarchistic slapstick comedians. They fed the homeless, and goofed on the rich and powerful. There was an insouciance about them that I identified with.

This young Black Panther was not unfriendly. He liked the piece, he said. But I should be careful about what I say in the newspapers. Some things were not meant for broad distribution. Perhaps I should clear things with the Panthers in Oakland the next time I wanted to write something about them. They had enough problems at the moment, trials and tribulations, literally everywhere. After I had been mildly reprimanded, this brother stood and walked out the door. I had been chastened and warned, and now this young dude was moving on. I went back to the apartment on Turk and Divisadero, about half a block away, and I told everyone what happened. Charlie and Sujenna laughed uproariously. Sarah seemed more concerned for my well-being, understanding that these people meant business.

After I had told everyone this story, Sujenna handed me an envelope, and when I opened it up, there was a check for $150 inside of it, and a short note from Ross Wetzsteon, an editor at *The Village Voice* newspaper, thanking me for the piece about the Panthers and the IRA.

"My first paid publication," I said, as everything else had been poems or pieces of fiction in small-press magazines that paid you in copies, usually two of them.

"What are you going to do with the money?" Sujenna asked.

"I'm going to take Sarah out to dinner at that French restaurant that Charlie told us about the other day."

"L'Orangerie," Charlie said.

"Yeah, I'll blow it on that."

"For two people, plus a bottle of wine, a tip, etc., it will probably come to $150."

"Good, then it's decided," I said, and I booked a reservation for the following night. Thus my time in California came to a close with a publication in *The Village Voice*, a meeting with Hubert Selby in Los Angeles, and a sumptuous meal in a French restaurant that Charlie kept talking about. Years later, Charlie would become the main food critic for the *Los Angeles Times*, his name known everywhere for his knowledge of food the world over. When we got back to Turk Street, Sarah rushed to the bathroom, where she projectile vomited. So much for the romance of French cuisine and wine. Meanwhile, Sarah and I took another cross-country train, only this time we took the northern route, a big mistake, and the train became snowbound in the Rockies. It took us about a week to get to Chicago, whereupon we promised never to ride trains again.

"You have to overcome your fear of flying," Sarah said, "or else you'll never be able to function in this world."

Back on West 10th Street in New York City, the honeymoon had ended. There is nothing like a cross-country trip with another person to find out how much you loved them or not. I wound up going back to the Eighth Street Bookshop to work the graveyard shift from six at night until midnight. In the daytime, when Sarah was at work for the newspaper, I returned to rewriting the novel for Grove Press, the title changing from *Up Against the Wall* to *Gulfweed Voices*. I had taken the title from a long poem by British poet Basil Bunting, a protégé of Ezra Pound's. His poem was called *Briggflatts*, and was rich in language unlike most contemporary American poets, at least the ones I knew, who followed a dogged path laid down by Pound and William Carlos Williams, though more certainly the latter than the former.

Oddly enough as I grew fonder of Sarah, she was pulling away from me, going in another direction than I supposed for myself. Ever since I was arrested in New Hampshire, I had begun to shy away from drugs and more thoroughly embraced the traditional torments of alcohol and cigarettes. Sarah was beginning to take LSD, while I was hanging out in the various Village bars when my bookshop shift ended at midnight.

"It may be time to find a new place to live," she said, and so I started looking around and asking people. Paul, a regular at the Lion's Head and the editor on a Hearst publication about youth and popular culture, said that he would be going away for the summer, and I could stay in his place for two months until I found my own apartment somewhere.

Summer arrived early and New York style—hot and humid. June 27th came upon us during that streak of hot and humid days. The doldrums were in the air, but also an edge that I had not experienced in the Village before.

Christopher Street was crowded and noisy, and I sat in the backroom of the Lion's Head, sitting at some tables near the front windows. There was far more people and movement out those windows onto Sheridan Square. I was sat at the table with Ron and his wife Nicki, Paul and his assistant Nancy, Tom Weatherly who had just gotten off from work in the kitchen, Frank Harris, a two-bit cowboy actor in spaghetti westerns, who also shared a birthday with me, and a bunch of other people, drinking and thanking God for air conditioning. Sarah was back at the apartment, probably already asleep. There was a kind of disconnect between us, as if the thread that connected us had somehow been severed. Communication was abrupt and short, not personal and warm. She would ask: "When are you moving out?" I would answer monosyllabically: "Soon." That was the end of it. I did not get off from work until midnight, and then I needed to unwind, needed to go somewhere before going home, so I often did not get back to the apartment until the early morning hours, at which time Sarah would be waking up, going off to her work at the newspaper up the street.

Paul and Nancy had eaten some hamburgers and now joined a bunch of us at the two tables near the windows.

The Stonewall riots—later upgraded to the Stonewall Rebellion—was taking place just beyond those windows in the Lion's Head. None of us had any idea how important this all would become. Christopher Street was ablaze with spontaneous rebellion, cops and rioters pounding away at each other, total anarchy on the street. Watching the Stonewall riots, it was almost like watching a 3-D newsreel. For the next couple of nights, the same scenario unfolded as evening progressed. For most of my gay friends, they date the beginning of Gay Rights to June 27, 1969, when that riot broke out at the Stonewall Inn, several doors down Christopher Street from the Lion's Head. Each night we sat at those same tables, watching the evening unfold with skirmishes, arrests, I think there may have even been some tear gas and other more drastic police actions. At the end of it, Gay Rights were born. Almost overnight *The Village Voice*, located at the corner of Christopher Street and Seventh Avenue South, shifted its editorial focus from Greenwich Village bohemia to becoming the vanguard of this new movement, a position it would hold through the next decade and beyond. Though I was an actual witness to one of the most important moments in late 20th century American cultural history, I witnessed it from the box seats of the Lion's Head, amid the drunken Irish-American journalists, the sports hacks, the public relations flacks, the failed writers, and the human wrecks of alcoholism, as young men in high heels, pink boas streaming behind them, faces made up to look like Greta Garbo or Marlene Dietrich, raced back and forth across Sheridan Square. "Patrons and passers-by attacked the police with rocks, bottles, and firebomb," Greg Robinson wrote in *The Encyclopedia of New York*. There was nothing to stop someone who had enough determination and tinted mascara to get through to the next decade and beyond. When the dust settled and the garbage trucks and the sanitation workers carted off the debris, the riot had turned into a rebellion. A new movement had been born.

In 1969, Gil Sorrentino hooked me up with the agent that he and Cubby used, someone at Sterling Lord, the agency which handled Jack Kerouac, who had just died. But even this high-powered agency couldn't get Grove Press to cough up with a contract for my manuscript, even though I had been told that the press wished to publish my book. When it seemed as if it never would come, that I might be better off withdrawing the manuscript, a contract arrived. Both Gil Sorrentino and Ross Feld were relieved for me. Part of the logjam had to do with Grove moving from University Place at 11th Street to new, larger, flashier quarters at Bleecker Street near Broadway.

Once I had my contract, I went around the corner to Broadway, stepped in St. Adrian Company bar, showed Bruce Bethany my contract and asked him for a tab. It would be my first—and it would turn out last—bar tab. But initially he was quite agreeable with the arrangement, warning me that he cut writers off sooner than painters if they didn't pay the tab in a timely fashion. I agreed to the terms and then, like Joel Oppenheimer at the Lion's Head, I began to drink myself to death and oblivion. I did this quite seriously, programmatically, and nightly. I ate all my meals—usually only one a day in the evening—at the bar, and occasionally I bought drinks and meals for other people. I was nothing if not grandiose, and though I didn't know it at the time, a big people pleaser, trying to win over their friendship by buying them drinks or those meals. Very soon my tab had become out of hand.

Sarah and I had parted ways, and so I was once again living here and there, although I managed to get a little stable when Paul, the pop music editor I knew from the Lion's Head, let me stay in his two-room apartment on West 10th Street, between Bleecker and West 4th, just off Sheridan Square. He had gone off to Berkeley, where he was from, as he had been working as a glossy magazine editor for Hearst, and now he was re-thinking what he wanted to do, after quitting his editorial position at the magazine. He had attended Berkeley with Jerry Greenberg, my junkie poet friend, and Charlie Perry, who had just been my roommate in San Francisco the year before. Paul's assistant was Nancy, Gauloise smoking, wine-drinking, poetry-reading, tall and elegant, beautiful and young, and out of work now that Paul had left the magazine.

Quickly she managed to get work at Grove Press, so I now had a spy in the House of Grove, and Nancy would tell me the real deal about what was going on at my putative publisher's. Nancy was upset that Paul had gone off to California, and I would commiserate with her, as she lived just down the block from his apartment, though mostly I was at St. Adrian Company, trying to make my tab as large as I could by drinking and eating there nightly. To put this into perspective, Max's Kansas City was famous for offering tabs to artists who drank there, some of them like Andy Warhol, running the tab into six figures and then paying for it with his creative work. Thus Mickey Ruskin (Max's owner) became an early collector of Andy Warhol, John Chamberlain, Dan Flavin, Donald Judd, and a host of other artists who paid their bills with their art. Everyone knew, though, that the bar owners got the better of that deal, and yet the artists were perfectly happy to accommodate them this way. My goal was to be as amazing as Andy Warhol in running up my tab, but of course I lacked his collateral. I was a writer, not a painter. Painters became Picasso, and millionaires; writers became Apollinaire, their pockets filled with poems, blood dripping from the bullet holes in their heads. I was hardly the ideal candidate for a bar tab in downtown New York.

Before summer's end, Bruce Bethany put me on notice, I either paid up my tab or I was cut off.

In short succession, Ross Feld lost his job at Grove Press, and then Gil Sorrentino was let go. I began to be moved from editor to editor, including Fred Jordan and Dick Seaver, although these were legendary editors, none of them had the enthusiasm for my writing that Ross and Gil had. Nancy, my friend from the Lion's Head, had become Grove's publisher Barney Rossett's assistant, and so she was able to tell me what really was going on at the press. They were overextended, after moving from University Place to Bleecker Street, and then building the business from publishing into filmmaking. Barney had commandeered a small movie theater on Bleecker Street near LaGuardia Place, and was showing the films he either produced or was distributing in the US. These were good films, and I saw lots of them during those days. But this was not a money-making operation, as beyond Greenwich Village and a few other enlightened spots in America, no one was going to pay money to see art-house films from South America and Europe.

Barney Rossett was considered unstable and unpredictable. He was reputed to use speed, and I knew that he had a bar in his office because I had been inside of it when he was not there, and I drank a few bottles of his beer because, as I reasoned with Nancy, he was such a cheap bastard and had given me such a piss-poor advance on my first novel. Though I had never formally been introduced to him, even after I had signed a book contract with his press, I often saw him late at night in the Lion's Head or more likely the 55 bar, one or two doors over, which was known locally as the bar-car on the D train, i.e., it was a serious dive for serious Village alcoholics. Sometimes I saw Barney sitting there, with Nancy sitting next to him, matching him drink for drink, as she was able to do quite well. Later, after he wandered off, she came into the Lion's Head, and if she felt like it, might tell me what was happening at my publisher's.

Away from Grove Press, Ross Feld had his first book of poetry taken by Jonathan Williams at the Jargon Society, and Gil Sorrentino's fiction career was taking off, a whole series of his books about to be published. Neither had suffered artistically from being let go from Grove Press, though I am sure it made paying the rent more difficult. When Gilbert Sorrentino left Grove Press, they lost one of their best editors; Gil had worked arduously on Selby's masterpiece, *Last Exit to Brooklyn*, for many years, meticulously helping his friend to make it the best book possible. Selby had told me, when I met him in Los Angeles the year before, that Gil had been instrumental in shaping Alex Haley's *Autobiography of Malcolm X* into publishing shape, too. Now Gil would write his own books and do freelance editing. Ross, his young assistant and my good friend, would find work as a freelance developmental editor and writer. It was shortly after he left Grove that Ross also began his long affiliation with *Kirkus Reviews*, the publishing magazine which reviewed important books before they were about to come out and was read by other review outlets to see what was being talked about within the trade and in New York City.

Somewhere around this time Gil moved from the East Village, where he had lived most of his adult life, with the exception of his time in Brooklyn. He found an apartment in the new Westbeth artists and writers complex near the West Side Highway and the North River. He and Joel Oppenheimer were now neighbors and still friends, though that would change soon after Gil published his novel, *Imaginative Qualities of Actual Things* (1971), a corrosive satire about the downtown art and literary scenes, and one in which an unflattering portrait of Joel in the guise of Leo Kaufman emerges. Leo is a great poet who has wasted his life on booze and hanging out on the downtown scene. Gil had published his first novel *The Sky Changes* in 1966, and that was followed by *Steelwork* (1970). He was also publishing his poetry with Black Sparrow, and he had a beautiful, book-length prose poem called *Splendide-Hotel*, that had come out with New Directions.

My manuscript would still be published, I was told, but just when it would be published no one had any idea. Nancy tried to find out what was happening. But there was no clear policy on what was going to happen to the novel. Eventually it wound up with a pile of other unpublished manuscripts on Dick Seaver's desk. I went by to speak to him about what was happening, but he wasn't expecting me in his office at that moment, had never met me before, and the meeting did not go well. We got into a shouting match, and I was asked to leave, which I did, slamming the door behind me. Later, I was told that Dick was a former boxer, and he looked fit and hearty, but I was twenty-three years old, and not afraid of anyone. Afterward, I was told by Nancy, that he admired my guts for coming in there and talking to him like that, not being afraid of his reputation and his position in the press. I think he was prepared to take the manuscript forward, but then he left the press, and shortly after that, the press more or less folded for a time, though Barney would soon again resuscitate the corpse of his publishing empire, if not the dead art of poetry, like Hugh Selwyn Mauberly tried to do in Ezra Pound's poem.

At Paul's two-room apartment on West 10th Street, there were nonetheless thousands of books and record albums. I would read *Under the Volcano* by Malcolm Lowry, as well as Henry Miller's books, most of which Paul had, as Miller was a friend of his father's, and in fact Paul planned on visiting Uncle Henry in Big Sur when he was in California for a visit. He had told me that he wanted to ask the old master what he should do with the rest of his life now that he was no longer a glossy magazine editor. Nightly I listened to Paul's vast record collection, starting with James Taylor's first album which came out six or seven months earlier, but invariably I wound up listening to Miles Davis' new electronic jazz. Davis' redefinition of what jazz was seemed like the most fitting for this time, even more than my love of Thelonious Monk, whose music I listened to more selectively, almost religiously, as a way to put me back in a frame of mind to write and be creative. Thelonious Monk's music was a spiritual point for me, whereas Miles Davis conveyed my own edginess beautifully, and I walked around the Village with a kind of strut, a young street guy with a book contract, the son of a Hell's Kitchen tough guy, as Irish as Milo but looking like a downtown Italian. The changes were everywhere, in Sheridan Square, with the new openness and boldness of the gay community; with the new voices coming out of the feminist movement; with the Black voices everywhere. The will to change was upon me, and I needed to do something differently.

I spent my mornings on West 10th Street near Sheridan Square and my evenings near lower Broadway, hanging out at the St. Adrian Company where Harry Lewis was the bartender and people like Jerry Roth, from Seymour Krim's workshop, hung out, along with Bill Amidon and some other writers from the prose workshop. Even though I no longer lived with Sarah, we did see each other, and she even came by Paul's apartment once. At other times, I went to Nancy's up the street near Sixth Avenue, where she experimented with French cuisine taken from Elizabeth David's cookbooks. We'd drink excessive amounts of Greek wine and smoke copious amounts of Gauloises cigarettes, the studio apartment on Milligan Place thick with the smoke in the air. When Nancy was sufficiently drunk, she would cry over Paul, her boyfriend whose flat I stayed at, and then she would read aloud from John Berryman, asking me what I thought. I liked the way she read Berryman, but he seemed too formal for my tastes then, though eventually I came to like many of his quirky later poems, which often reminded me of Ezra Pound, only even crazier. It was thanks to Nancy that I even came to read Berryman at all, as she was persistent in defending his poetry to me, as we smoked and drank, ate and got so drunk that we became sober, and got drunk again.

Nancy was a beautiful young woman. I say that she was a young woman, but she was probably a year or two younger than I was, so maybe I mean that she was still inexperienced compared to the cynical people whom I knew. I visited her apartment several times a week during that period, though we never made love. She was still too hung up on Paul, the person still controlling their relationship from miles away. I once heard it said that the person who is least involved controls a relationship, and that was true with Paul and Nancy. Still, I stopped by to smoke French cigarettes, listen to poetry read aloud, and eat Davidian lamb shank stew, giving her a critique afterwards of her cooking, which really was superb.

I tried to get her to read some poetry from Frank O'Hara or Joel Oppenheimer, the latter whom she knew quite well from the Lion's Head. But her poetry tastes were wedded to John Berryman. Finally, I wandered off. I went to Max's, then I wended my way down Broadway to St. Adrian Company, at least before I got cut off for not paying my tab in a timely manner. I ambled into the Eighth Street Bookshop. Sometimes I walked down to the Battery or across the Brooklyn Bridge into Brooklyn or I walked uptown to Central Park, walking around there for hours on end. Around midnight, I walked back downtown, aimlessly. The summer was hot, the air was thick with humidity, the nights were long, the apartment too hot to stay in. I sat in the backroom of the Lion's Head, listening to Joe Heaney play his little squeezebox, singing as mournfully as a Moorish dirge in Andalusia, only the music was Irish, and so was Joe. I wandered over to the East Village, and down Second Avenue to Ron and Nicki's place on First Street, but they were not home, so I walked back through the Bowery, across the bleakness of Bleecker Street, stumbling past the stumble bums, nearly one of them myself, except that I had a book contract in my pocket and my friends were artists and writers. Otherwise there was really no difference between me and the Bowery bums.

One evening I decided that I needed my green overcoat which was still at Sarah's apartment down the road from Paul's flat. Her apartment was further west, two blocks away, just across Hudson Street. I walked over, reeling and rocking, went up the tenement stairs in the hallway, and knocked on her door. When she answered, seeing my state of mind, she wisely said that she wasn't going to let me in, that I could get my overcoat another time. (It was the end of summer, so the coat was certainly not an essential piece of clothing.) She had someone there with her. Out in the hallway, she tried to talk me down off my emotional ledge, but it was a circular narrative in my head. I punched her in the face. Then I pushed through the door, and went stomping through the rooms of her railroad flat. In the front parlor, I came face to face with her new boyfriend, who was tall and wiry, quite a few years older than I was, wearing the requisite long dark hair and the droopy mustaches. I thought of him as a kind of replacement part for me, a better version, if you will. Right away he took offense at my presence, either said or did something, but the next thing I knew, I had socked him in the mouth, and this very tall man, ten years my senior, had fallen to the floor. Sarah broke a wine bottle on my head, and I went reeling out of the apartment with my green overcoat in hand. I hardly had any need of the green overcoat. The police had been called. I packed up and left Paul's place immediately. I contacted Rudy Wurlitzer and asked if he had any suggestions of where I might go. He suggested that I go to Provincetown, Massachusetts until things cooled down. He gave me the name of two painters whom he knew there, and said I should call them when I got to town. I managed to hitch a ride into New Haven with Clark Whelton and Bart Gerald, two writers from the prose workshop, and then I took a train to Providence, whereupon I hopped on a bus going to Cape Cod.

In the autumn about twenty P-town residents gathered in the Howard Johnson's parking lot to be a small part of the two-million citizens protesting the war in Vietnam that particular day. I remember meeting the poet Alan Dugan there, and thinking he was Robert Lowell until someone straightened me out right away, and then I remembered him reading, many years earlier, in the garden of the New School in the Village, and how taken I was with his poem about the boxer, Hurricane Jackson. It was a beautiful autumn day as the people gathered in the HoJo parking lot. Others drove by, honking their horns in support of our quixotic enterprise.

When the Provincetown protest ended, people walked off, going for Portuguese kale soup or schooners of beer, fish to get from the town pier and then to cook later, or off to studios to write or paint, the salt air on our tongues and in our hair and everywhere that day. The writer Howard Zinn once observed that in 1965, after the US's initial bombing of North Vietnam, a hundred people gathered on the Boston Common to protest that military action. He went on: "On October 15, 1969 the number of people assembled on the Boston Common to protest the war was one hundred thousand." In Provincetown there were not one hundred thousand people, only twenty of us.

I did not hear Miles Davis that afternoon in front of HoJo's in Provincetown, nor Thelonious Monk or any sort of music that I associated with my own journey through the decade. While American cities burned, naked children ran down unpaved roads in Vietnam after napalm had literally burnt the clothes off their backs. The war ground on. The cities still burned. Social justice was ignored. I walked back to my room on the water's edge along Commercial Street, my Portuguese landlady greeting me hello. I walked up the back stairs to my efficiency apartment that faced the harbor. The tide rolled in. I was alone. The sun had set already. The coolness of night ran across the harbor. Gulls screeched. Night had come. I had just enough money to get me through the winter, and then I would need to rethink what it was I wanted to do. I stood on the landing in front of my apartment and looked at the enormity of the sky, turning inky black with night. I had no idea what it was that lay beyond that horizon. I put the key in the door to my second-floor flat, and went in and lay down on my unmade bed. I stared at the ceiling.

Amid the assassinations of the 1960s, there was this nameless, faceless American ronin, the masterless samurai who is legend in comic strips and martial arts films. What those films and strips don't tell you is that the ronin's actions are often a sign of failure of imagination. Violence is always a failure of imagination, although I did not know that at the time. This memoir has been nothing if not about the imagination in all of its permutations. What I remember is this: I left after I threw the punch and got the bottle broken over my skull. When I woke the next day, I quickly packed my bags and left the city, if not for good, then until the dust settled. The streets were clear. As I walked to a friend's place to get my ride out of town, I realized my enormous failure from the night before. This was not a literary badge of honor the way Seymour Krim's failures were. It was a complete and total failure of my imagination, coming face to face with my own human limitations, my own mortality. Relationships end; people move on, even when it is the time of the assassins.

M. G. STEPHENS (Michael Gregory Stephens) is author of over 30 books, including such classic works of fiction—and long out of print—as *Season at Coole* and *The Brooklyn Book of the Dead*, both of which novels have had a lot of critical response in book chapters on Stephens' work. Along with *Kid Coole* those novels comprise *The Coole Trilogy*. In the last few years, he has published the novels *King Ezra* (2022), about the poet Ezra Pound, and the third novel in *The Coole Trilogy, Kid Coole* (2022), a boxing novel about the underbelly of multicultural America. In 2025, Spuyten Duyvil is publishing three new books by M. G. Stephens: his memoir about the Poetry Project's early days, *When Poetry Was the World*; the linked stories, *Come On, Eileen*, about Eileen Coole, an Irish poet, who meets, falls in love, and marries the jazz musician and political activist Santiago Santa, and their long exile of 20 years in Algiers, Algeria. Finally, Spuyten Duyvil has brought out a collaboration between Stephens and Brooklyn artist Archie Rand, *Popeye, Unchained*, 85 unrhymed blank-verse mostly sonnets, about Popeye and Co., along with 85 collages by Rand. In 2021, Stephens published the hybrid work of fiction, poetry, and nonfiction, *History of Theatre or the Glass of Fashion*, about an out of work actor who lands the part of Hamlet. He is also the author of *Jesus' Dog*, stories, that was published by Paycock Press in 2024. Michael Gregory Stephens lived in London for 15 years, and during that time, from 2003 to 2006, he researched and wrote a doctorate at the University of Essex in Colchester, England, on the origins of the Poetry Project at St. Mark's Church in-the-Bowery. He was 20 years old when he first showed up at the newly opened Poetry Project in the East Village in 1966. Forty years later, he received his doctorate on those early days in downtown New York. *When Poetry Was the World* is girded by that research, although it is also a straight up memoir full of stories from the 1960s on the Lower East Side.